# The
# Ruler
# Who
# Serves

Discovery Books

# The
# Ruler
# Who
# Serves

Ray C. Stedman

Word Books, Publisher
Waco, Texas

*The Ruler Who Serves*

Discovery Books are published by Word Books,
Publisher in cooperation with Discovery Foundation,
Palo Alto, California.

ISBN 0–87680–840–2
Library of Congress catalog card number: 76–20972
Printed in the United States of America

# Contents

# 1

# The Way of the Cross

The Gospel of Mark emphasizes in particular two aspects of Jesus' life. In the first half, Mark shows us Jesus as "The Servant Who Rules," * the One who came as the servant of man—healing, helping, comforting, restoring—yet with such power and authority that, along with the disciples, our eyes are opened finally to see that he is nothing less than the Lord of glory himself.

But no sooner have we discovered who Jesus was and is, than, incredibly, he begins to speak about his death. This was startling to the disciples, and it represents the turning point in the Gospel of Mark. From this point, Jesus is on his way to Jerusalem, to the darkness of Gethsemane's garden, to the judgment hall of Pilate, to the whipping post, and to the bloody cross. Yet on the way, as we shall see, he is still ministering to men, still healing, still comforting, still cleans-

---

* *The Servant Who Rules* is the title of the book containing our studies in the first half of Mark's Gospel. This chapter, "The Way of the Cross," forms the end of that book, and the beginning of this one, as it sets forth the focal point of Jesus' ministry and life.

ing, restoring, and blessing men. But now he is "The Ruler
Who Serves," and this is the theme of the last half of our study
in Mark.

If you will permit me just a word of outline so that you can
see where we are going—this last half falls into two major
divisions. Beginning with chapter 8, verse 34, and continuing
through chapter 13, we have what I am going to call "The
Way of the Cross." It is our Lord's preparation of his disciples for the dire event that awaits him as he comes into
Jerusalem. Chapters 14 through 16, which conclude the Gospel, relate the events of the cross and the resurrection. In the
division we begin now, The Way of the Cross, there are also
two subdivisions: first, our Lord's preparation of the disciples
at Caesarea Philippi, at Capernaum, and proceeding down the
Jordan River valley; second, the events at Jericho, on the
Mount of Olives, and in Jerusalem. First we will consider only
that part of his preparation of the disciples which took place
at Caesarea Phillippi, in the north of Galilee at the foot of
Mount Hermon. After Jesus had announced the cross to his
disciples, had been rebuked by Peter, and had rebuked him in
turn, Mark tells us,

> And he called to him the multitude with his disciples, and said
> to them, "If any man would come after me, let him deny him-
> self and take up his cross and follow me" (Mk. 8:34).

This is our Lord's outline of the process of discipleship.
Here, in his own words, we look at what it means to be a disciple. The very fact that our Lord called the multitudes together *with* the disciples has raised questions in people's minds.
Many have wondered if this indicates that he was seeking to
make disciples, i.e., evangelizing, or was he simply telling his
own disciples what it will mean to live as disciples? In other
words, can you be a Christian and not be a disciple? Is discipleship a second stage of Christianity? Are there many

Christians, but only relatively few disciples? *Can* you be a Christian and not be a disciple? These are very important questions, and our Lord himself will answer them for us.

Let us focus our attention now on these simple but very crucial words of Jesus, whereby he gives us the process of discipleship. There are three steps, he says. First, "If any man [anyone] would come after me, let him deny himself . . ." Notice that he does not say, "Let him hate himself." He is not asking us to deny our basic humanity, our personhood. If you take it that way, you have missed the point. And he is not telling us that we are to abandon ourselves. We cannot get outside of ourselves in any way. So we must understand what he does mean by this phrase, "deny himself," which is the first step of discipleship.

## No Connections

The word "deny" means to "disavow any connection with" something, to state that you are not connected in any way with whatever is in view. Interestingly enough, it is the very word used to refer to Peter's denial of Jesus a little later on. As he was standing in the courtyard of the high priest, warming himself at a fire, a little maiden asked him, "Do you know this man?" Peter denied that he had any connection with Jesus, said he did not know him, and affirmed his disavowal with oaths and curses. Thus he denied his Lord. That is exactly the word Jesus chooses when he tells us that if we are going to come after him, we must first deny ourselves.

It is important also to understand that he does not mean what we usually mean by "self-denial." By this we usually mean that we are giving up something. Many people feel it is only right to deny themselves something during Lent—to give up various bad habits, like wearing overshoes in bed. But Jesus is not talking about this kind of "self-denial." He is never concerned about what we *do* so much as with what we *are*. Therefore he is not talking about giving up luxuries, or even necessities, but about denying *self,* which is entirely different. Denying *self* means that we repudiate our natural feelings about ourselves, i.e., our right to ourselves, our right to run our own lives. We are to deny that we own ourselves. We do not have the final right to decide what we are going to do or where we are going to go. When it is stated in those terms, people sense immediately that Jesus is saying something very fundamental. It strikes right at the heart of our very existence, because the one thing that we, as human beings, value and covet and protect above anything else is the right to make ultimate decisions for ourselves. We refuse to be under anything or anybody, but reserve the right to make the final decisions in our lives. This is what Jesus is talking about. He is not talking about giving up this or that, but about giving up ourselves. Paul says the same thing Jesus is saying: "You are not your own; you are bought with a price" (1 Cor. 6:19–20). If you are going to follow Jesus, you no longer own yourself. He has ultimate rights; he has Lordship of your life. So you no longer belong to yourself; he must make those final decisions when the great issues of your life hang in the balance. This is what Jesus means by, "If anyone would come after me, let him deny himself"—deny our self-trust, deny our self-sufficiency, deny our feeling that we are able to handle life by ourselves and run everything to suit ourselves.

Some years ago I read an article entitled, "The Art of Being A Big Shot," written by a friend of mine, a prominent Christian businessman named Howard Butt. Among many other good things he said, were these words which I quote because they are so illustrative of what our Lord means here:

It is my pride that makes me independent of God. It's appealing to me to feel that I am the master of my fate, that I run my own life, call my own shots, go it alone. But, that feeling is my basic dishonesty. I can't go it alone. I have to get help from other people, and I can't ultimately rely on myself. I'm dependent on

God for my very next breath. It is dishonest of me to pretend that I'm anything but a man—small, weak, and limited. So, living independent of God is self-delusion. It is not just a matter of pride being an unfortunate little trait, and humility being an attractive little virtue; it's my inner psychological integrity that's at stake. When I am conceited, I am lying to myself about what I am. I am pretending to be God, and not man. My pride is the idolatrous worship of myself. And that is the national religion of Hell!

That is a very eloquent explanation of what Jesus means when he says, "If anyone would come after me, let him deny himself. Let him give up his rights to run his life, let him submit himself to my leadership, to my Lordship." And this is fundamental to all discipleship. There can be no discipleship apart from it.

The second step immediately follows: "Let him deny himself, *and take up his cross* . . ." What does "take up his cross" mean? Well, I am sure these words were almost totally incomprehensible to the disciples. They did not know what he meant. To them, the cross was but a vague, hazy blur on the horizon of their minds. They did not understand where Jesus was heading. But he knew. And he knew that after the awful events which were to come in Jerusalem, after the terrible, searing pain of those days was answered by the joy and the glory of resurrection, they would think these words through again and begin to understand what he meant. We who live on this side of the cross find it easier to know what he meant.

Still, many people think that a cross is any kind of trial or hardship you are going through, or any kind of handicap you must endure—like a mother-in-law, or a ding-a-ling neighbor, or a physical handicap. "That's my cross," we say. But that is not what Jesus means. He himself had many handicaps, many difficulties and trials, before he came to his cross. So it is not merely handicap or difficulty or trial. The cross was something different. The cross stood for something in the life of Jesus connected with shame and humiliation. It was a criminal's cross on which he was hung. It was a place of degradation, where he was demeaned and debased.

## Welcome the Shame

And so the cross stands forever as a symbol of those circumstances and events in our experience which humble us, expose us, offend our pride, shame us, and reveal our basic evil—that evil which Jesus described earlier: "Out of the heart of man come evil thoughts, fornication, theft, murder, adultery, coveting, wickedness, deceit, licentiousness, envy, slander, pride, and foolishness." It is the cross which brings this out. It is any circumstance, any incident which does this to us. Jesus says, if we are a disciple, we are to welcome it. That is his meaning. "Take up your cross, accept it, glory in it, cling to it, because it is something good for you. It will reduce you to the place where you will be ready to receive the gift of the grace of God." That is why the cross is so valuable to us.

This does not mean only the big things in our life; it is the little things as well. Do you feel hurt when someone forgets your name? Do you get upset when a cashier will not cash your check? Does criticism hurt, even when you know it is justified? Are you rankled when you lose at tennis or golf? All these are minor forms of the cross at work in our lives. The Lord's word is that if we are going to be a disciple, we are not to be offended by these things, we are not to get upset about them; we are to welcome them.

You can see how radical this approach to life is, how different it is from the way the world would tell us to act. The world says, "Escape. Avoid the situation. Or if you can't avoid it, then strike back. Get angry, get even, offend in turn. Get upset about it." But the word of Jesus is, "If you're going to be my disciple, deny yourself, and take up your cross."

Then the third step is, "Follow me." This really means,

"Obey me." Is it not remarkable that it takes us so long to understand that if disobedience is the name of the game before we are Christians, then certainly obedience is the name of the game after we become Christians. It must be. I am amazed at people who say they are Christians, but then blatantly, and even pridefully, acknowledge that they do not follow the Lord, do not do what he says. Now, we all struggle with this. I myself fail at this many times. Our Lord is not talking about perfection as a disciple; he is simply telling us what discipleship means, what it involves. It involves following him. It means choosing to do or say what Jesus commands us to do or say, and what he himself did—and looking to him for the power to carry it through. This is what following him means. It is what it meant to the disciples. They obeyed him, and they were taught to look to him for whatever it took to make it possible. In the feeding of the multitude, he told them to feed the crowd, and they did. But he had to supply what it took.

This is what Christianity is all about. The Christian life is following Jesus, doing what he says—like, "Love your enemy. Pray for those who hurt you. Forgive those who offend you." Those are not merely wise and helpful words; they represent a way of life our Lord is setting out before us, one to which we are expected to conform in the moment when we least feel like it. When we do not feel like obeying or forgiving or praying, he tells us to do it anyway. "Be kind to the ungrateful and the selfish." I struggle with that one. I do not want to be kind to people who are ungrateful or selfish, but that is what the Lord says to do. "Bear one another's burdens. Freely you have received, freely give." "Follow me," means obeying these and all the many, many other exhortations of Scripture.

In the original Greek, these steps are stated in the present, continuous tense. That means, "Keep on denying yourself, keep on taking up your cross, keep on following me." This is not the decision of a moment but a program for a lifetime, to be repeated again and again whenever we fall into circumstances which make these choices necessary. This is what it means to be a disciple. Discipleship is denying your right to yourself and taking up the cross, accepting these incidents and circumstances which expose pride and conceit, welcoming them, and then following him, doing what he says to do, looking to him for the power.

This is not always a very appealing course, is it? I am sure that it must have struck these disciples and the multitude with very solemn and serious impact. In fact, John tells us that at this point many turned and went back and followed him no more, because these words seemed to them harsh and demanding. We can always be grateful that our Lord never has invited any to come after him without letting them know what would be involved. He told them straight from the shoulder what they would be getting into. And he does this with us. He is not interested in anybody's becoming a Christian or attempting to live as a Christian on false terms. He wants us to understand that this is going to shatter us, change us, make us into a different kind of person. It is bound to. If it has any meaning in our lives at all, it is going to revolutionize us utterly, right to the very core of our being. He makes this very clear, right from the start.

And then he goes on to give us the motive which will move us in this direction: "For whoever would save his life will lose it; and whoever loses his life for my sake and the gospel's will save it" (Mk. 8:35).

That is motive enough, certainly. Who is not interested in saving his life? That is, making it worthwhile, making it complete and full and rich, worth the living. We all want that. Deep down within us, every one of us has a hunger for life and a desire to find it to the full extent of what it was designed to be. This is what Jesus is talking about. "If this is what you want," he says, "I'll tell you how to acquire it." There are two attitudes toward life which are possible, and you can have only one or the other. One is: save your life now, i.e., hoard it, clutch it, cling to it, grasp it, try to get hold of it for yourself, take care of yourself, trust yourself, see that in every situation your first and major concern is, "What's in it for me?" That is one way to live, and millions are living that way today. All of us, at one time or another, do this.

The other attitude is: lose it, i.e., fling it away, disregard what advantage there may be for you in a situation and move out in dependence upon God, careless of what may happen to you. Paul says, "I count not my life dear unto myself." Abraham obeyed God, went out on a march without a map into a land he knew not where, apparently careless of what would happen to him. And his neighbors reproached him, rebuked him for not caring about himself. This is to be a way of life, Jesus says. Trust God, obey him, and put the responsibility for what happens on his shoulders. This is the way of life Jesus offers—to lose your life like that.

## A Fundamental Law

And he says there are only two results which can follow. If you save your life, if you cling to it, hoard it, get all you can for yourself, then, without a doubt, Jesus says, you will lose it. This is not a mere platitude, a truism. He is stating a fundamental law of life. It is absolutely unbreakable. Nobody can break this law. If you save your life, says Jesus, you will lose it. You will find that you have everything you want, but you will not want anything you have. You will find that the life you tried to grasp has slipped through your fingers, and you have ended up with a handful of cobwebs and ashes, dissatisfied, hollow and empty, mocked by what you hoped to get.

There are many who are proving this today. Ask the man who has everything, "Are you happy?" He may answer, "Yes, I am. I've got everything I want, I can do anything I like, I can go anywhere, at any time. I've got all the money I need. Yes, I'm happy." But if you press him, "Does that mean you're satisfied with yourself, content with your life, fulfilled, con-

vinced that your life has been worthwhile, and that you can
go to your grave with a deep sense of having invested your
life well?" If you press, you will ultimately get the answer,
"No, something's missing. I thought these things would fulfill
me, I thought they'd satisfy that deep craving down inside, but
they haven't. It is still there. I still feel there must be something beyond, something more that I haven't got." This is
what Jesus is talking about. "Save your life, and you will
lose it."

"But lose your life for my sake and the gospel's," says Jesus;
"lose your life by means of giving yourself away in my cause,
giving up your right to yourself, taking up your cross and following me, and you will save it." You will not waste it; you
will save it. You will find a contentment and satisfaction, an
inner peace, and a sense of worth about your living. You will
discover, not just in heaven someday but right now, that even
though you may not have all the things others have, your life
will be rich and rewarding and satisfying.

There is an illustration I often use to point up this truth. I
can imagine the scene when the apostle Paul appeared before
Nero, the Roman emperor, to give answer to the charges
against him. There is the emperor, in his royal robes, seated
upon a throne. His name was known throughout the empire.
But nobody knew of Paul, this obscure little Jew, bald-headed,
big-nosed, bandy-legged, totally unimpressive in his physical
appearance—he says so himself in his letters. And he was a
leader of an obscure, heretical little sect that was known only
as troublemakers. Nobody had heard of Paul, while everybody
had heard of Nero. But the interesting thing is that now, two
thousand years later, we name our sons Paul, and our dogs
Nero.

This is God's part in the work of discipleship. Jesus did not
come to call us to ultimate barrenness, weakness, darkness, and
death; he called us to life, to richness, to enjoyment, to fulfillment. But he has told us that the way there means death. Dis-

cipleship ends in life, not in death. It ends in fulfillment and satisfaction. But the only way that we can find it is by means of a cross.

## Profit and Loss

The final issue is set forth in our Lord's words in the closing part of this paragraph:

> "For what does it profit a man, to gain the whole world and forfeit his life ["soul" is the Greek word]? For what can a man give in return for his life [soul]?" (Mk. 8:36–37).

Oh, these questions of Jesus—how they search us! What does it profit a man to gain the whole world and lose his own life? This question hangs over our whole generation, as it has hung over every generation since that day. What good is it to get all the things you want and have nothing with which to enjoy them if you have lost your life in the process? Is it not the very essence of wisdom, if you are going to invest time and money and everything you have, to make sure you are able to enjoy the result when you are through? Would anybody knowingly build a house contrary to all the zoning ordinances and building codes, with the certain result that when he has spent all his money and built the house, he will not be permitted even to move in? What foolishness that would be! And yet how many lives are being built without any consideration of this question, or any dealing with the God who stands at the end of the road? This is why Jesus asks, "What would it profit a man to gain the whole world and lose his life? What can a man give in return for his life?"

Many years ago archaeologists dsicovered the tomb of Charlemagne, great Eighth- and Ninth-Century king and emperor of France. When the tomb was opened, after being closed for centuries, the men who entered it found something amazing. They found certain treasures of the kingdom, of course. But in

the center of the large vault was a throne, and seated on the
throne was the skeleton of Charlemagne with an open Bible
on his lap and a bony finger pointing at the words, "For what
shall it profit a man, if he shall gain the whole world and lose
his own soul?" What a tremendous lesson from history to
those of us who follow!

Jesus not only asks this question, but he also points out that
there is no way we can cheat:

> "For whoever is ashamed of me and of my words in this adul-
> terous and sinful generation, of him will the Son of man also be
> ashamed, when he comes in the glory of his Father with the holy
> angels" (Mk. 8:38).

That is, deeds and not words will tell the story. It is not what
we have said we believe; it is how we have acted that will make
the difference. Somebody once asked me, "What does it mean,
to be ashamed of Jesus? My son, who is in high school, said
to me the other day, 'You know, Dad, I've learned a way of
saying grace before I eat in the cafeteria so that nobody knows
about it. I just bend over and tie my shoe.' Is that being
ashamed of Christ?" Yes, it is, in a way. But I do not think
little incidents like this are what our Lord is talking about. We
are all tempted, at times, to be nervous about professing to
be a Christian, or to manifest it only in certain circles. And
the temptation is not wrong. What our Lord is talking about
here is a settled way of life which outwardly expresses con-
formity to Christian truth but inwardly adopts and follows and
conforms to the values of the world. This, he says, is what will
be revealed in that day. Remember that at the close of the
Sermon on the Mount he said, "Many shall come to me in
that day, and say, 'Have we not done many mighty works in
your name? Have we not cast out devils, and preached in your
name?' And I shall say, 'Depart from me, I never knew you,
you workers of iniquity.' "

So there is the answer to the question we asked at the beginning: Can a person be a Christian and not a disciple? Well, you can come to Christ, and all who come are given life if they mean it when they come. But it is clear that unless you take up the work of discipleship, this life is given in vain. Paul calls this "accepting the grace of God in vain." Only those who are disciples enter into an abundant life. Now, we are not all good disciples at all times; there is much of failure. And our Lord has made provision for failure in our lives. But he is talking about the heart. What is your aim? What do you really want of your life? Do you want to live it for yourself or do you want to live it for him? That is really the question.

C. S. Lewis gathers all this up very well in these words from *Mere Christianity:*

> God is going to invade this earth in force. But what is the good of saying you are on His side then, when you see the whole natural universe melting away like a dream, and something else —something it never entered your head to conceive—comes crashing in; something so beautiful to some of us, and so terrible to others, that none of us will have any choice left? For this time it will be God without disguise; something so overwhelming that it will strike either irresistible love or irresistible horror into every creature. It will be too late then to choose your side. There is no use saying you choose to lie down when it has become impossible to stand up. That will not be the time for choosing; it will be the time when we discover which side we have really chosen, whether we realized it before or not. Now, today, this moment, is our chance to choose the right side. God is holding back, to give us that chance. It will not last forever. We must take it or leave it.

This is what Jesus said to the men of his day. Becoming a Christian is not easy. It is radical. But it is the only way to life.

# 2

# The Glory That Follows

One of the most dramatic events in Scripture—ranking perhaps only after the crucifixion and resurrection of our Lord —is the transfiguration of Jesus. This event follows his announcement of the cross and of the way of discipleship. It deals with what it would cost to be his disciples, and what the blessings would be as well. It is evident from Mark's text that Jesus knew the transfiguration was coming; he announced it at least six full days before it happened. He had led the disciples, all twelve of them, to the foot of Mount Hermon in order that they might prepare for this event.

I believe that the transfiguration took place on Mount Hermon, that beautiful snow-covered mountain north of the sea of Galilee. The account begins in the closing verse of chapter 8 and continues through the first thirteen verses of chapter 9. Right at the beginning we are struck by the fact that our Lord tells the reason for this event before it ever happened. In the first verse of chapter 9 we read,

And he said to them, "Truly, I say to you, there are some standing here who will not taste death before they see the kingdom
of God come with power" (Mk. 9:1).

Some liberal commentators have misunderstood this passage,
feeling that Jesus was predicting that the time of his second
coming would be within the lifetime of people who were alive
at that moment. Many have been troubled by this interpretation because, obviously, his second coming did not take place
then. Some have even gone so far as to say that Jesus was
mistaken as to the time of his second coming.

But if you link this statement with what immediately follows, it is clear that Jesus is referring to the transfiguration.
He is saying that some who were there at that moment would
not taste death until they saw this manifestation of the kingdom of God, of his coming, and of the glory of his reign in
power. This then provides a clue as to what the event means:
it was a preview of the coming glory. Jesus states that it will
be a manifestation of his coming into his kingdom with power.
On subsequent occasions, as he teaches the disciples on the
Mount of Olives and other places, he speaks of that coming
with power: "You shall see the Son of man coming in the
clouds of heaven with all his mighty angels." Notice that he
has just referred to this at the close of chapter 8:

> "For whoever is ashamed of me and of my words in this adul-
> terous and sinful generation, of him will the Son of man also
> be ashamed, when he comes in the glory of his Father with the
> holy angels" (Mk. 8:38).

That is the event they are to preview, as Peter himself makes
very clear to us. Our Lord chose Peter and James and John to
be with him on the mountaintop. Of the three, only Peter later
refers explicitly to this event in his writings, clearly and carefully in 2 Peter 1:

For we did not follow cleverly devised myths when we made
known to you the power and coming of our Lord Jesus Christ,
but we were eyewitnesses of his majesty. For when he received
honor and glory from God the Father and the voice was borne
to him by the Majestic Glory, "This is my beloved Son, with
whom I am well pleased," we heard this voice borne from
heaven, for we were with him on the holy mountain (2 Pet.
1:16–18).

Thus Peter confirms that our Lord is here giving a foreview
of what it will be like when he comes again in glory with all
his holy angels.

## To End in Glory

Also—and this is very important—Jesus implies that this
event is what awaits the believer at death. Notice that he says,
"There are some standing here who will not taste death before
they see the kingdom of God come with power." The implication is that ordinarily it *is* by tasting death that the believer sees
the kingdom of God come with power. Other passages confirm
very clearly that when a believer dies, the event which meets
his eyes, and into which he steps as he leaves time and enters
eternity, is this coming of the Lord with his angels. This is
why in Jude it is recorded "that Enoch in the seventh generation from Adam prophesied, saying, 'Behold, the Lord came
with his holy myriads . . .' " (Jude 1:14). This is the event
that awaits the believer at death.

But here our Lord says that some who were then present
would see this before death. It is clear, then, that the reason
the transfiguration happened was to encourage the disciples.
He had just announced the way of the cross and his coming
death in Jerusalem. So he gives them this incident to strengthen
their faith, to encourage them that it was not going to end in
darkness and disaster; rather, it would end in triumph and
victory and glory. And it is intended to encourage us when we,

too, must take up our cross. We can be assured it is not going
to end in disaster but in glory.

Now let us look at the event itself:

> And after six days Jesus took with him Peter and James and
> John, and led them up a high mountain apart by themselves;
> and he was transfigured before them, and his garments became
> glistening, intensely white, as no fuller on earth could bleach
> them. And there appeared to them Elijah with Moses; and they
> were talking to Jesus. And Peter said to Jesus, "Master, it is
> well that we are here; let us make three booths, one for you and
> one for Moses and one for Elijah." For he did not know what to
> say, for they were exceedingly afraid. And a cloud overshadowed
> them, and a voice came out of the cloud, "This is my beloved
> Son; listen to him." And suddenly looking around they no longer
> saw any one with them but Jesus only (Mk. 9:2–8).

A remarkable event! There are four dramatic occurrences
in this account that immediately rivet our attention. First, there
is the glorious change in the person of the Lord himself. Suddenly, as they were with Jesus there on that mountain, his
countenance altered, Matthew tells us. His face began to shine,
his garments became white, and his whole being radiated
glory. It is interesting to read how some of the critical commentators treat this incident. One says that Jesus was praying
on the mountaintop when suddenly the sun broke through the
clouds and shone upon him—in that brilliant sunlight he appeared to the disciples to be supernaturally changed. Well,
that is all very well in accounting for his change, but it does
not explain Moses and Elijah nor the other events that happened. It is clear from this account (and from Matthew's and
Luke's also)—Mark is careful to point out—that this is a
supernatural change. No fuller on earth could produce this.
This even exceeds the claims of the soap and detergent ads of
our day. There is no whiteness like this whiteness, and the
writers are very careful to make that plain.

## No Need to Die

Well, what happened to Jesus? We can only understand this when we see that what he did was to slip back into eternity, in a sense—back into his pre-human glory, which he refers to later in his great prayer recorded in John 17. He prayed, "Father, glorify thou me in thy own presence with the glory which I had with thee before the world was made." This is the glory which now is suddenly revealed to these three disciples. It is evident, therefore, that our Lord did not have to die. That is one of the meanings of the transfiguration; he had no reason to pass through death. He could step back across the boundary of time into eternity without passing through death. We must die; he did not need to. He could step back into glory at any time, and here he did so.

Although John does not give us an account of the transfiguration, I am sure this is what he is referring to in his Gospel when he says, "The Word became flesh and dwelt among us . . . and we have beheld his glory." Though he does not tell us where, it was undoubtedly this moment on the mountain that he remembered.

The second thing that grips us is the account of the heavenly visitors. Moses and Elijah appeared and were talking with Jesus. Is it not interesting that the disciples seem to have no difficulty at all in recognizing instantly who these men were? Jesus did not say, "Now Peter, James, and John, I'd like to have you meet Moses and Elijah." No, they knew instantly who they were. There will be no need for introductions in glory; we will know immediately who people are. So this account gives us something of a preview of what heaven will be like.

But why Moses and Elijah? Many have puzzled over that. Why not one of the other prophets—Isaiah or Jeremiah; why not David or some of the other great leaders of the Old Testa-

ment—Abraham, perhaps, or Noah? But it was particularly
Moses and Elijah who appeared with Jesus on the mountain.
I think the commentators are right when in general they say
this is because these two were preeminently the representatives
of the Law and the Prophets, those two great divisions of the
Old Testament which pointed forward to the coming of Messiah—Moses, the great law-giver; Elijah, the first, and in some
ways the greatest, of the prophets.

## Two Ways to Heaven

It is also interesting to note that these two men represent
the two ways by which men have entered heaven. Moses entered through the normal, natural process of death. No man
was present when Moses died, but God buried him, the Old
Testament says. And yet here Moses is—his body lying in
some unmarked grave on a mountaintop beyond the Jordan
River, but he himself in a resurrected body—present on the
mountain with Jesus. Elijah, on the other hand, was one of
two men caught up to heaven without death. We have the
dramatic story in the Old Testament of Elijah's ascension into
glory—caught up in a fiery chariot without passing through
the normal process of death.

We have a prediction of this same phenomenon in the New
Testament. Believers today normally enter into glory through
death, as Moses did. But Paul tells us that the generation of
Christians who are living on the day of the Lord's return
shall not taste death. In 1 Corinthians 15:51, he says, "We
shall not all sleep, but we shall all be changed, in a moment,
in the twinkling of an eye, at the last trumpet." And in 1 Thessalonians 4:16–17, "For the Lord himself will descend from
heaven with a cry of command, with the archangel's call, and
with the sound of the trumpet of God. And the dead in Christ
will rise first; then we who are alive, who are left, shall be
caught up together with them in the clouds to meet the Lord

in the air; and so we shall always be with the Lord." So there are two ways by which believers can enter into glory, and these are represented here by Moses and Elijah.

I am always intrigued by the fact that Moses is here because it means that he finally made it into the Promised Land! In the wilderness, because he got angry and disobeyed the Lord, God told him that he would not be permitted to lead the children of Israel into the Promised Land. He could see the land, but he could not enter. But that prohibition was only in time. Now, in eternity, he was permitted to enter the land. And here he is on the mountaintop. I can just see him looking all around, looking over that land, and saying, "So there it is! I've been wanting to come here for ages, and I've finally made it!"

Luke tells us that they spoke of the exodus of Jesus, of his departure from Jerusalem. They discussed together how he would leave the earth by means of a cross and a resurrection. I am sure these three disciples were so perturbed by the splendor and the glory and the strangeness of this scene that they did not recall all that they heard, which is too bad, for what a conversation this must have been! How I wish we could have been present and heard them discussing these things. Moses perhaps discussed how Jesus was the fulfillment of all those sacrifices which the law demanded—all the lambs and calves and bulls and goats which were killed as a picture of the suffering One who would come. Elijah, as one of the prophets, perhaps spoke of the longings of men, the hungering after a leader, a conqueror, a Savior; and of the predictions of the prophets that One was coming who would bear our transgressions, enter into our heartaches, and free us from ourselves. Such must have been their discussion.

The third element of great interest in this account is the proposal which Peter makes. After hearing these men discussing the strange events together, Peter, in his usual manner, interrupts: "Master, it is good for us to be here. This is tremendous! Let's make three booths and live here. Let's settle down here and make this our world headquarters. We'll make one booth for you, one for Moses, and one for Elijah." He evidently has in mind that they would transform that mountain into the headquarters for the world-wide reformation movement that was going to start. They would operate right from that mountain, as the center of all activity.

Well, that shows how foolish he was, and how little he understood what Jesus had been trying to tell him. In fact, Mark, who undoubtedly got this account from Peter's own lips, indicates that the motive which led Peter to speak was that of fear. He said, "They were exceedingly afraid." Someone has said that there are only two kinds of speakers: those who have something to say and those who have to say something! Peter was someone who just had to say something. He blurted out whatever came to his mind without stopping to think whether it made sense or not. So he makes the proposal that they make this their headquarters for a great campaign to take over the world.

## Shekinah

But he scarcely had gotten the words out when he was interrupted, and the fourth dramatic event occurred. Suddenly, they were overshadowed with a cloud. Matthew tells us it was a bright cloud, a very bright, shining cloud. It is my conviction that it was the identical cloud mentioned in the Old Testament, which hovered over the tabernacle during the day—the glory of God, called the "Shekinah." They heard a voice speaking out of the cloud, saying, "This is my beloved Son; listen to him." There is no doubt that this is a correction of Peter's brash statement. The Father himself is saying, "Peter, do not put Jesus on a par with Moses and Elijah. You listen to *him.* He is the one of whom Moses and Elijah spoke. He is the one who fulfilled all the predictions of the prophets and the sacrifices of the law. Listen to him; this is my beloved Son."

There are three occasions in the New Testament when the

voice of God spoke directly from heaven concerning the work of Jesus. One was at his baptism, when he began his ministry. There the words were addressed to Jesus himself: "Thou art my beloved Son, in whom I am well pleased." It is evident that the voice came to launch the ministry of Jesus. Here we have the words addressed to the disciples to correct a mistake they were making. The third account occurs in John's Gospel, chapter 12, just before the cross in Jerusalem. Jesus said in prayer to the Father, "Glorify thy name." And a voice spoke from glory and said, "I have glorified it, and I will glorify it again," referring to the cross immediately to follow. There the voice came to complete the testimony of the life and ministry of Jesus. So three times we have the voice of the Father from heaven: to launch his ministry; to correct a mistaken idea about him; and to complete the testimony that Jesus gave by his life and ministry.

Mark ends this account by telling us that as the voice spoke, suddenly the scene faded. They were returned to the normal situation. As he puts it so beautifully, ". . . they no longer saw any one with them but Jesus only." Jesus himself remained after the glory had faded.

In the next section we have the discussion that ensued as they were coming down the mountainside:

> And as they were coming down the mountain, he charged them to tell no one what they had seen, until the Son of man should have risen from the dead. So they kept the matter to themselves, questioning what the rising from the dead meant. And they asked him, "Why do the scribes say that first Elijah must come?" And he said to them, "Elijah does come first to restore all things; and how is it written of the Son of man, that he should suffer many things and be treated with contempt? But I tell you that Elijah has come, and they did to him whatever they pleased, as it is written of him" (Mk. 9:9–13).

There are two features of importance in this account. First, the verbal quarantine which Jesus laid on these disciples.

Once again he forbade them to tell anyone what they had seen—even the other disciples, evidently. Of course, our immediate question is: why does he do this? Why does he show them his transfiguration but then tell them not to say anything? If you look closely, you can see two reasons. One, of course, was because their information was incomplete. They needed the resurrection in order to understand all that was happening. Without that resurrection, the whole process would be incomplete. They apparently had ignored all he had said about the resurrection, and so now he tells them not to say a thing until after it occurs. Without that, their message would be meaningless—a hopeless jumble which would only mislead men and set them on the wrong track.

And second, it is very clear that their understanding was also incomplete. They kept the matter to themselves then, but questioned "what the rising from the dead meant." They did not understand that. Probably, like Martha in the eleventh chapter of John, they linked this with the great resurrection yet to come, referred to in the Old Testament, when all the dead should rise. They could not make the connection and did not see it as referring to the resurrection of Jesus.

## The Wrong Order

If we understand this, we will understand why they asked the question about Elijah which follows immediately: "Why do the scribes say that first Elijah must come?" If you put all that back into context, you can see that they felt what they had just seen on the mountain—Elijah and Moses speaking with Jesus—was the fulfillment of the prophecy of Malachi that Elijah must come. But their problem was: he had come in the wrong order. He had not come first, before Messiah appeared, and they could not understand that. They said, "Why then do the scribes say that first Elijah must come?" The emphasis is on the word "first." They are confused, they do not know how to tie the resurrection into this, and they do not know how to explain that Elijah did not come first and restore all things before Messiah appeared.

So Jesus' answer to them is very instructive. We must observe it very carefully because he does something rather unusual here. He says to them, "Elijah *does* come first to restore all things; and how is it written of the Son of man [referring to himself, not Elijah], that he [Jesus] should suffer many things and be treated with contempt?" If you notice, he has carefully changed the subject from Elijah to himself. Then he says, "But I tell you that Elijah has come, and [notice the tense] they *do* to him [not they "did" to him, as it is translated] whatever they please, as it is written of him." Who is he referring to there? The Son of man, not Elijah. That agrees with what he has just quoted—that he would suffer many things and be treated with contempt. It is not written anywhere of Elijah that he would suffer many things and be treated with contempt. That is a reference to Messiah. So Jesus is saying, "Elijah will come; but as to Messiah, they are doing to him whatever they please, as it is written of him." He changes the focus of their question from Elijah to himself.

What does all this mean? Well, he is really saying that the issue is not Elijah's coming first. What will happen first will be the suffering and death of Messiah. This is what they ought to focus on. This is what he is trying to drive home to them, what he seeks to impart to them again and again through this whole process of teaching them before the cross. He emphasizes it here again: "The cross must come first."

Now, it is true that in Matthew's account he refers to John the Baptist as having fulfilled, in some secondary way, this promise concerning Elijah. And you remember that at the announcement of the birth of John the Baptist, an angel appeared to his father saying that his wife would have a son, that his name should be called John, that he would go before the Lord to prepare his way, and that he would do so in the spirit and power of Elijah. Our Lord indicates that in some way John was a fulfillment of that prediction about Elijah. But he was not Elijah; he came in the spirit and power of Elijah. He was not the reincarnation of Elijah, but was engaged in the same type of ministry Elijah had.

But our Lord also makes clear here that before Messiah appears in glory, in his second coming, Elijah will indeed come first; "Elijah does come first," he says. But the important thing now for the disciples is the shame and suffering of the cross, which Jesus himself would experience.

## At the Foot of the Mountain

The account closes with the story of an event which took place at the foot of the mountain: the curing of the demon-filled boy. As we will see in a moment, it is linked with the transfiguration. Mark begins by recounting the impotence of the disciples:

> And when they came to the disciples, they saw a great crowd about them, and scribes arguing with them. And immediately all the crowd, when they saw him, were greatly amazed, and ran up to him and greeted him. And he asked them, "What are you discussing with them?" And one of the crowd answered him, "Teacher, I brought my son to you, for he has a dumb spirit; and wherever it seizes him, it dashes him down; and he foams and grinds his teeth and becomes rigid; and I asked your disciples to cast it out, and they were not able." And he answered them, "O faithless generation, how long am I to be with you? How long am I to bear with you? Bring him to me" (Mk. 9:14–19).

We need to be a bit understanding with these disciples. They *were* faithless, as Jesus said, but they had a difficult problem facing them here. It is clear that this boy was a very difficult case to handle, as even Jesus later acknowledged. It was not a simple case of epilepsy, as it might appear on the surface. It is true that the symptoms recorded here are the classic symptoms of epilepsy. But the Bible records instances of epilepsy,

as well as of demon possession, and distinguishes between
them. Here it is clear that the problem was being caused not
by epilepsy but by demon power. Today we know that many
things can happen in the brain to cause such convulsive fits. A
brain tumor or certain chemical imbalances can cause them.
Certainly it is not at all incredible that demon power could
cause a seizure of this type. So this is not epilepsy; it is really
caused by a very powerful demon, one of what Paul calls
"principalities and powers, wicked spirits in high places," a being of incredible craft and power, evidently extremely difficult
to dislodge, as we shall see. This is perhaps one reason why
Jesus asked the boy's father, "How long has this been going
on?" This was his clue that it was a very difficult case to
handle. Furthermore, while Jesus was away, these disciples
were surrounded by unbelieving scribes who were opposing
them in everything they did, arguing with them over everything. It was a very difficult situation, and they were unable
to cast out the demon.

Why did they fail? I think it is clear that our Lord put his
finger on the basic reason: their lack of faith. But notice something very important. They did not fail because they did not
expect anything to happen. They were surprised when it did
not happen. They expected the boy to be delivered. They had
seen people delivered before from demons when they said the
word in Jesus' name. But this time it did not happen. So faith
is not merely a sense of expecting something to happen. That
ought to be clear from this account. What is it, then? Jesus
said their problem was that they were faithless. Yet they did
have a kind of faith: they expected that something would happen. What did he mean?

### Faith in a Formula

Well, if you think it through, you can see what had happened. They had faith, but it had changed from faith in God
to faith in the process they were following. They thought that

if you said the right words and followed the right ritual, the demon would have to leave. Without their even realizing it, they had transferred their faith from confidence in a God who can act to a formula that can bring it about. This is what we often do. We get to thinking that it is the words we say, or the way we say them, or what is happening in our lives, which is the real reason things happen—rather than the God who acts. Jesus reproved them for this and said their faith must be in God himself, if it is to be a fresh and vital faith.

The power of that kind of faith is exemplified by our Lord himself:

> And they brought the boy to him; and when the spirit saw him, immediately it convulsed the boy, and he fell on the ground and rolled about, foaming at the mouth. And Jesus asked his father, "How long has he had this?" And he said, "From childhood. And it has often cast him into the fire and into the water, to destroy him; but if you can do anything, have pity on us and help us." And Jesus said to him, "If you can! All things are possible to him who believes." Immediately the father of the child cried out and said, "I believe; help my unbelief!" And when Jesus saw that a crowd came running together, he rebuked the unclean spirit, saying to it, "You dumb and deaf spirit, I command you, come out of him, and never enter him again." And after crying out and convulsing him terribly, it came out, and the boy was like a corpse; so that most of them said, "He is dead." But Jesus took him by the hand and lifted him up, and he arose (Mk. 9:20–27).

Notice the father's unbelief. He said, "If there is anything you can do—*if* there is—please help us." That is simply an honest statement of where he is. Jesus gently challenges him, "If you can! No, that's never the problem; the problem is, 'If *you* will believe.' If you will believe not only in a God who can, but in a God who will, it can be done. Nothing is impossible if you'll believe. The problem is in you, not in me."

Immediately, the man did a beautiful thing. He said these
words which have been the encouragement of many since: "I
do believe; help my unbelief!" Out of the honesty of his weakness, he cast himself on the Lord. "Yes, Lord, I do believe; but
I feel my unbelief and I don't know how to handle it. You
make me believe." That kind of faith is small, but it is like a
grain of mustard seed—it is able to move mountains. The
moment he said those words, the moment he cast himself in
his weakness back on the Lord, that was all God wanted. Our
Lord spoke the words, and his son was delivered. You can see
the severity of the case. It was with reluctance, even at the
command of Jesus, that this spirit came out of the boy. It
cried out, convulsed him, then left him as dead. But Jesus
picked him up by the hand and restored him.

In the last verses we get the secret of that power:

> And when he had entered the house, his disciples asked him
> privately, "Why could we not cast it out?" And he said to them,
> "This kind cannot be driven out by anything but prayer" (Mk.
> 9:28–29).

He does not mean prayer uttered at the moment, because Jesus
himself did not pray when he cast out this demon. He is not
talking about a certain kind of prayer that you say at the
moment you want to relieve somebody of a demon. No, what
he means is a lifestyle of prayer. "This kind cannot be driven
out except by a heart which is kept fresh and alive and in
touch with God by a life of prayer." That is where Jesus' power
came from. He was always in touch with the Father. He was
always drawing upon his Father's power. He always walked in
reliance upon God. He referred every event of his existence to
the God who indwelt him, and he prayed consistently and
constantly to the Father in expectation of his working. This is
what he is talking about—maintaining a fresh and vigorous
relationship with God and trusting in him. This is a life of
prayer.

Now let's go back to the beginning for just a moment. Remember that Jesus said, "There will be some standing here who will not taste death before they see the kingdom of God come with power." What had these disciples just seen? They had seen the kingdom of God come with power into the life of a father and his boy. And what made it come? Well, as Jesus points out, it was the presence within of a living God and a reliance maintained by a constant communication with him. This is what permits the kingdom of God to come with power, right now, in the midst of our daily affairs. When we understand that, we can say with Paul, "If God be for us, who can be against us?"

# 3

# The Child in Our Midst

In the section of Mark we are studying, we have been watching Jesus gently but very firmly leading his disciples to face up to the implications of the cross. We Christians often make much of the joy and love and the glory of Christianity. But usually we avoid the thought of suffering and persecution, of discipline, and of dying. Much of the church today is trying to avoid these implications of the cross. But Jesus makes clear to his disciples, and to us, that there is no glory without the cross—no cross; no crown.

Following the events of the transfiguration and the healing of the demon-controlled boy, Mark tells us that Jesus passed through Galilee again on his way to Capernaum, and he stresses the teaching ministry of the Lord to his disciples:

> They went on from there and passed through Galilee. And he would not have any one know it, for he was teaching his disciples, saying to them, "The Son of man will be delivered into the hands of men, and they will kill him; and when he is killed, after three days he will rise." But they did not understand the saying, and they were afraid to ask him (Mk. 9:30–32).

It is evident from the account that our Lord deliberately avoided the crowds as they went back toward Capernaum. They took the back roads in order not to be seen because he wanted to spend time with these disciples. All through the Gospels you see that his target was these twelve men. He was intent on conveying truth to *them* above all else.

In this announcement of the cross, a new element is added which has not appeared before: "The Son of man will be delivered into the hands of men." The word translated "delivered" really means "betrayed." It is the very word used later to describe the betrayal of Judas. Here is a strong hint to these disciples that the way the Lord would be turned over to his enemies would be by an act of betrayal. What this meant to Judas, we are not told. But Jesus clearly knew what would happen from the very beginning.

### The Fear of Knowing

Mark records that the reaction of the disciples was evidently one of distaste. They did not like this. Mark tells us they did not understand the saying and didn't even ask him anything about it because they were afraid. It is easy to read that as though they were afraid that if they asked him he might rebuke them. But the striking thing is that Jesus never once rebuked anybody for asking a question. He rebuked his disciples often for not having much faith, for remaining unbelieving in spite of all they had seen; but he never rebuked them for asking questions. Yet even though this puzzled them, and they did not understand what he meant, they did not ask him about it. So it is clear that what held them back was the fear of knowing more about it. When someone has brought up a subject that you do not like, have you ever said, "Well, let's not talk about it," or, if you were expected to ask questions, have you refused because you did not want to know any more about the subject? We all tend to bury our heads in the sand at times, to think that if we do not look at something, it will go away. But Jesus

confronts them continuously with this inescapable fact of the
cross, even though they do not want to see it.

They did not want to look at it more closely because of the
feeling that was already in their hearts, which Mark goes on
to reveal to us:

> And they came to Capernaum; and when he was in the house
> he asked them, "What were you discussing on the way?" But
> they were silent; for on the way they had discussed with one
> another who was the greatest. And he sat down and called the
> twelve; and he said to them, "If any one would be first, he must
> be last of all and servant of all." And he took a child, and put
> him in the midst of them; and taking him in his arms, he said
> to them, "Whoever receives one such child in my name receives
> me; and whoever receives me, receives not me but him who sent
> me" (Mk. 9:33–37).

Our Lord evidently knew what these disciples had been
talking about. Even though he had not been close enough to
them to hear, he sensed what was going on. So when they
get into the house at Capernaum, he asks them, "What were
you discussing on the way?"—a simple, normal question—but
he is met by embarrassed silence because, as Mark tells us,
they had been discussing who was the greatest among them.
Somehow that did not sound right in the presence of Jesus. It
would be wonderful if we always had this awareness that what
we say and think is being done in his presence. It would make
us feel differently about many things, I am sure.

We are not told how this argument came about. I rather
suspect, because of the context, that it was occasioned by the
events of the transfiguration. James, Peter, and John had been
chosen to go up on the mountain with the Lord and observe
this marvelous sight. And Jesus had strictly charged them to
tell no man what they had seen. I believe they kept this charge
and did not say anything to the other disciples. But it is quite
possible, you know, to keep a secret in such a way as to make

everybody agog to find out more. When Peter, James, and John came back, the others probably asked, "Well, tell us, what happened up there?" And they said, "Oh, we're not permitted to say. One of these days perhaps we might be able to tell you, but you ordinary disciples are excluded from this for now." And then, of course, the argument readily arose as to who was greatest. They began to debate and argue with one another.

## No Rebuke for Ambition

To answer this, Jesus gave them a marvelously revealing statement. He told them the truth about ambition, and it is a very helpful word. He called them to himself and said, "If any one would be first, he must be last of all and servant of all." Notice something very significant about that. He did not on this or on any other occasion rebuke them for wanting to be greatest. Never does he take them to task because of their desire. God has somehow built into every human heart the desire to succeed at whatever we do, in whatever terms we may conceive success to lie. He did not rebuke them, for this is part of our humanity—to want to succeed, to be the greatest. What he did do was to tell them the true way to greatness. "It is not by seeking to be first," he said; "It is by a willingness to be last. It is not by getting people to serve you; it is by becoming a servant of all."

What he is really saying is that there are two kinds of greatness, two kinds of ambition. There is the ambition to be approved and applauded by men, and the ambition to be approved and applauded by God. These are as different as night and day. There are those who want to gain fame and attention and influence and power. The measurement of the ambition to be great before men is always: "How many serve me? How much power do I exercise over others? How wide is the extent of my influence? How far has knowledge about me traveled?" Who of us has not suffered many times this desire to be known, to be admired, to be considered important and great in the eyes of men?

But Jesus points out that true greatness is never found there. The measure of true greatness is: "How many do I serve? How many am I willing to minister to? How many can I help? This is the mark of greatness in the eyes of God. This is enduring greatness. You can see how disparate these two views are, how widely they diverge. Christianity is a radical faith! It will completely revolutionize our thinking. It is exactly the opposite of the natural instincts of the heart. This is why, as we grow as Christians, we learn more and more to act not according to the way we feel, the natural inclination, but to act on a quite different basis. Our natural inclinations will simply get us deeper and deeper into trouble. Though we may achieve a form of greatness in the eyes of men, it is nothing but a temporary, momentary achievement.

To drive this lesson home, in that wonderful way Jesus had, he called a child to him and, putting his arms around the lad, he said to the disciples, "Whoever receives one such child in my name receives me; and whoever receives me, receives not me but him who sent me."

This is a beautiful scene. I can see it in my mind's eye, as I hope you can—our Lord, with his arms about this boy. We are not told whose boy it was. But one thing is clear: it was not a child especially prepared for this occasion. It was not a Sunday school boy who had just been taught all the right answers to give; he was just an ordinary lad. He may have been Peter's son, because this probably took place in the house of Simon Peter, where Jesus made his headquarters in Capernaum. If so, he was doubtless full of the old man, and therefore a rascal. Jesus gathered this little rascal in his arms and, standing there with the boy, said to his disciples, "Now, true greatness is modeled on this."

Then he went on to bring out in three remarkable ways what we could call "the lessons of a child," or to put it in other words—the real marks of greatness, what to be ambitious for in your life. It is right that you should be ambitious, but be ambitious for the right things. The first is found in these words: "Whoever receives one such child in my name receives me." The important words there are, "in my name." The motive for receiving such a person, such a small, unimportant child, is that it is done as unto the Lord—done in his name. It is not done because something of great value may come to you because of the child; it is something you do regardless of whether you receive any benefit in doing it because it is done in his name. I like William Barclay's comment on this, and would like to share it with you:

> Now, a child has no influence at all. A child cannot advance a man's career, nor enhance a man's prestige. A child cannot give us things; it's the other way around. A child needs things. A child must have things done for him. And so Jesus is saying, "If a man welcomes the poor, ordinary people, the people who have no influence, and no wealth, and no power, the people who need things done for them, then he's welcoming me. And more than that, he's welcoming God." *

Surely the first mark of greatness is that you learn increasingly to have no respect of persons. We must learn to welcome people simply because they are people, to take no consideration of whether they can do something for us or not, and not to be concerned whether knowing them enhances our own prestige, so we can drop their names where it will do us the most good. We are simply to be interested in people because, potentially at least, they are sons and daughters of God himself. That is the first mark of the children of God.

## Don't Quench the Spark

This is illustrated in the next section by John, quite unwittingly. At this point, Mark says, John interrupted Jesus:

---

* William Barclay, ed., *The Gospel of Mark* (Philadelphia: Westminster Press, 1957), p. 231.

John said to him, "Teacher, we saw a man casting out demons
in your name, and we forbade him, because he was not following
us." But Jesus said, "Do not forbid him; for no one who does a
mighty work in my name will be able soon after to speak evil of
me. For he that is not against us is for us" (Mk. 9:38–40).

It is difficult to tell exactly why what Jesus was saying
brought this to John's mind. It was probably the mention of
the phrase, "in my name." It suddenly recalled to John an incident which had taken place not long before when he and
some of the other disciples had seen a man casting out demons
in the name of Jesus. John said, "Teacher, when we saw him,
we told him to stop, because he didn't belong to our school;
he wasn't following us." This is a typically human reaction, is
it not? How many times do we instinctively react this way
when we hear of someone who is achieving something? We
say, "Well, it can't be good, because he didn't go to our
seminary," or, "He doesn't belong to our denomination," or,
"I've never heard of him before." So we tend to reject him. I
think John was troubled by the success of this individual. What
appalled him was that this man was actually succeeding in
casting out demons! It was not a phony ministry, he was no
fake; he was doing it, and doing it in the name of Jesus! Yet
John had never heard anything about the man before. It was
his very success that troubled John.

So he asked Jesus, "Did we do the right thing?" Our Lord's
answer is, "No, don't forbid him. For one who does a mighty
work in my name will not be able soon after to speak evil of
me." What does he mean by that? He is implying that if this
man was actually casting out demons, then obviously there was
some faith in his heart. God does not respond to anything but
faith. And though no one knew much about him and what he
believed—and there may have been considerable error in what
he taught—nevertheless, the fact that God was answering him
and demons *were* being cast out in the name of Jesus indicated

that there was some reality about his ministry, that some spark of truth had gotten home to this man. Though he may have been mixed up in many ways, he was right to some degree. Jesus says, "When you see that, don't quench that spark. Don't reject people because they don't know everything yet, because they're still on the way, still learning. Don't forbid them to act; there is something of reality about them, and if you encourage them, you can lead them along and train them further and teach them more."

This principle has been amply demonstrated in many ways in our day. Many churches at the height of the "Jesus movement" turned their backs upon the young people who came to them—because they dressed strangely, had bare feet, wore beads, and had weird looking hairstyles. Many church people said, "We don't want this kind among us," failing to note the signs of true faith among these young people. Thus they missed out on the blessing of opening their lives to them.

I was involved in an incident not long ago which illustrates this principle. I saw an announcement in the newspaper of a meeting of the Gay People's Union at Stanford University. Two prominent speakers were featured—one a woman homosexual, a professor at San Francisco State University, the other a young man, also a homosexual who had been ordained to the ministry in the United Church of Christ. They were speaking on the subject, "Homosexuality and the Church." One of our interns and I went over to the meeting. We found about a hundred young people, with a few older ones here and there, fairly evenly divided between men and women. We listened an hour or so to these two speakers. The woman was very vitriolic. She denounced the church in almost every form and in every way. She said that it had to be destroyed, that it was the enemy of human liberty and freedom.

The young man was milder in his approach. He told of his own desire to find a place within the church, but of how, nevertheless, he found himself struggling because of the homo-

sexuality he endorsed, and of how he had been mistreated on
occasion because of misunderstanding on the part of others. I
could agree with a great many things he said about the church
and its weaknesses, and I noticed one thing in particular as he
spoke. He referred several times to Jesus and his ministry
with people. And it was true, exactly as our Lord said here, that
no one who uses his name will soon after be able to speak evil
of him. Whenever this young man spoke of Jesus, it was with
great respect and obvious admiration of his ministry.

After an hour or so of this, I felt that it was time to say
something for the other side. So I identified myself, spoke up,
and said, "I can agree with much that has been said about the
church, but I don't think you have come to grips with the real
issue—the stance of Christianity toward homosexuality. The
nearest you came was when this young man spoke of Jesus
and the woman at the well." He had brought out that Jesus
had not castigated her or denounced her, had not scorned her
and turned his back on her. I said, "Nevertheless, he did speak
to her about her condition—having lived with five husbands
and now living with a man who was not her husband. He then
offered her release, relief." I said, "I think this is the true
Christian position. Homosexuality is very injurious; it destroys
people. Jesus understands that, but he doesn't want to denounce people or drive them away; he wants to offer to them a
way out."

As I looked at that roomful of young people, I did not see
a room full of lesbians and faggots, though they were calling
themselves those names. I saw some spiritually hungry, mixed-
up, stunted, fragmented, and hurting young people—wanting
somehow to find the secret of life, thinking they had found it—
but on a wrong track and destroying themselves in the process.
Over and over Paul's words in Romans about homosexuals kept
coming into my mind: "They receive in their own persons the
due penalty of their error." The stance of the church toward
those who are involved in wrongful and evil things is never

to be one of denunciation. It is never to be one of stigmatizing and of rejecting. It is to be one of open-armed acceptance, but with an honest evaluation of what is going on and the offer of the way of release.

This is what Jesus is saying to his disciples. The mark of greatness is that you look not at a person's outward appearance, nor at the outward characteristics they manifest, nor even at the things they stand for, but that you see a human being who is groping after truth and life. And if the name of Jesus is respected in any way at all, do not quench that spark but feed it.

## More Serious Than Murder

The second mark of greatness follows immediately:

"For truly, I say to you, whoever gives you a cup of water to drink because you bear the name of Christ, will by no means lose his reward. [Do not stop there, for the sentence goes right on in the original language. "And . . ."] Whoever causes one of these little ones who believe in me to sin, it would be better for him if a great millstone were hung round his neck and he were thrown into the sea" (Mk 9:40–42).

Remember that Jesus speaks these words with his arms still around the little child. What he is saying is that the mark of true greatness in his kingdom is that someone takes humanity seriously and longs to see it develop rightly. The slightest ministry to a young believer is rewarded by God. Even a cup of cold water given in the name of Christ will never lose its reward. Every opportunity taken to help someone develop into fullness of health spiritually, as well as in soul and body, is to be rewarded by God. But on the other hand, any damage, any spiritual injury to a young Christian, is more serious than murder or physical injury: "Better for him that a great millstone be hung round his neck and he be cast into the depths of the sea, than to cause one of these little ones who believe in me to stumble."

I remember a number of years ago reading a short story by O. Henry in which he told of a little girl whose mother had died. When the father would come home from work, he would fix their meal, then he would sit down with his paper and pipe, put his feet up on the mantle, and read. The little girl would come and say, "Father, would you play with me?" And he would say, "No, I'm too tired, I'm too busy. Go out in the street and play." This went on for so long that finally the little girl grew up on the streets, and became what we would call a streetwalker, a prostitute. Eventually she died, and when, in the story, her soul appeared at the gates of heaven, Peter said to Jesus, "Here's this prostitute. Shall we send her to hell?" Jesus said, "No, no; let her in. But go find the man who refused to play with his little girl, and send him to hell."

Here in Mark's Gospel Jesus is saying that neglect is sometimes the greatest injury done to children and to young believers and that we must recognize this as a serious matter.

The third characteristic follows immediately:

"And if your hand causes you to sin, cut it off; it is better for you to enter life maimed than with two hands to go to hell, to the unquenchable fire. And if your foot causes you to sin, cut it off; it is better for you to enter life lame than with two feet to be thrown into hell. And if your eye causes you to sin, pluck it out; it is better for you to enter the kingdom of God with one eye than with two eyes to be thrown into hell, where their worm does not die, and the fire is not quenched. For every one will be salted with fire" (Mk. 9:43–49).

The third mark of greatness, as we can learn from thinking of children, is that the one who takes young people seriously must learn to start judging himself, the sin in his own life. Remember, this is uttered with his arms still around the child. He is saying that the mark of one who takes seriously the importance of spiritual growth is that he begins to judge himself,

deals drastically with himself. These words about cutting off
the hand and foot and eye are but an intensified and dramatic
way of saying what Jesus said on another occasion: *"First*
remove the beam that is in your own eye, and then you will
see clearly how to help another." The analogy he draws is
very clear and is taken from life itself. If you have an infected
arm that develops gangrene, it is threatening your very life,
and the doctors cannot do any more for you, there is only one
thing left to do: cut it off, amputate it. Your *life* is at stake.
Jesus uses that very dramatic analogy to tell us how serious
it is when we are involved in wrongful and hurtful attitudes
and actions, and what we must do about it. We must deal
drastically with these things; otherwise they involve us in hell.

The word used here for "hell" is "gehenna." Gehenna was
the name of a valley outside Jerusalem. It was the place where
some of the kings of Israel had offered their children to the
god Moloch to be burned with fire. It was a defiled place, and
it became the garbage dump of Jerusalem. Fires smoldered
there continuously; repulsive and ugly worms ate at the garbage. That becomes the symbol of the eternal waste of life.
When we read these words of Jesus about hell (By the way,
he spoke more of hell than any other person in the New
Testament), we must understand that when they are applied
to an unbeliever, i.e., one who resists and rejects the good
news of Jesus and dies an unbeliever, it means his whole life
is like that—wasted, a total loss. There is nothing salvageable
about it. He may have won the approval of men, may have
lived very comfortably, but at the end his life is a wipe-out, a
total loss, good only to be thrown on the garbage heap for
eternity. When these words apply to believers, as they do here,
he is speaking of partial loss. Some of our life is wasted,
squandered, lost; it is misused.

## The Salt of Self-Judgment

The way we avoid that loss and wasting of life is, as Jesus
said, to salt ourselves with fire, i.e., to judge ourselves. The

fire represents judgment in our life. He tells us to deal drastically with ourselves in this way, and, in this very helpful analogy he gives, he starts with the hand. To "cut off the hand," of course refers to eliminating the actual act that is wrong, the evil deed. If you have a dirty mind, a filthy mouth, stop thinking evil thoughts, stop using obscene terms. Deal with the hand, cut it off. If you are engaged in sexual wrong, stop it. If your attitude toward another is bitter and resentful, stop thinking that way. Stop saying the things you say about them. Deal with the act, cut it off. Otherwise you waste your life.

And then, if that is not enough, the foot has to be cut off. The foot is the symbol of the path that leads to evil, the approach to temptation—the circumstances that lead you there. You may have to change where you go and what you spend your time doing because you are confronted with temptation too strong for you to handle. Cut it off. It may be that you will have to limit the time you spend watching television, or stop watching certain programs, or not attend certain movies, or not read certain books, because these expose you to pressures which are too much for you to handle. Cut them off; otherwise you will waste your life.

Or it may be that the eye—the symbol of the inner vision, the pictures we see in our imaginations, the fantasies, the memories and dreams of the past which light the flame of temptation—must be plucked out. Jesus is saying that you must deal drastically with these things. They not only waste you, but they affect others. They *must* be dealt with. He concludes with these words:

> "Salt is good; but if the salt has lost its saltness, how will you season it? Have salt in yourselves, and be at peace with one another" (Mk. 9:50).

Salt, the salt of self-judgment, the chemical fire which purifies and cleanses, is good. Judge yourself, look at yourself, and evaluate what you are doing; learn to control yourself. But remember, it must be real; it cannot be phony. Salt which has lost its saltness is worth nothing. It must be real, genuine salt. And so, have salt in yourselves, and be at peace with one another. Remember how this account opens. A group of disciples are arguing as to who is going to be greatest—fighting, competing, rivaling one another. Jesus says that the remedy is to have salt in yourselves, to begin with yourself, to deal with your own weakness and not another's, to cleanse your own life and not another's. Start dealing drastically with the things which are wrong in your own life. For the marks of greatness in the kingdom of God are these: to learn to treat everyone the same, without respect of persons; to take life and humanity seriously, and be concerned to profit others, to build into their lives and strengthen them and not harm them or injure them; and to begin to judge yourself and deal drastically with the things in your own heart which are wrong. Such a person rises in stature and greatness in the eyes of God, and will be honored before the whole watching world.

# 4

# What About Divorce?

In the tenth chapter of Mark we have the account of a new journey our Lord took with his disciples, leaving Galilee for the last time. The first verse sets the scene:

And he left there and went to the region of Judea and beyond the Jordan, and crowds gathered to him again; and again, as his custom was, he taught them (Mk. 10:1).

This verse summarizes a rather extensive ministry our Lord had in Samaria and northern Judea after he left Galilee. It was during this time that he sent out seventy disciples, as earlier he had sent out the twelve, to go into all the villages and preach the gospel. Also, as John tells us in the tenth chapter of his Gospel, he made a quick trip to Jerusalem in the dead of winter and appeared at the feast of dedication. Having spoken at that feast, he left Jerusalem and came with his disciples now into the area on the eastern side of the Jordan River which Mark refers to as "beyond the Jordan." Here, in the region called Perea, he was ministering: "Crowds gathered

to him again; and again, as his custom was, he taught them."
During this time some Pharisees came to him, as Mark goes on
to tell us: "And Pharisees came up and in order to test him
asked, 'Is it lawful for a man to divorce his wife?'" (Mk.
10:2).

Mark is careful to point out the motive which brought them.
They came in order to test him. The Greek word used here
suggests that they were probing him, jabbing at him verbally,
attempting to stir up trouble, trying to catch him saying something which would allow them to provoke a crisis. Their hostility against him has intensified, and they are determined to
put him to death. So they select a very controversial question,
one which was bound to draw considerable interest on the part
of the people—the eternal issue of divorce.

## Two Schools of Thought

It is evident that they are trying to get him to make a choice
between the two views which were widely held in that day,
represented by two main schools of thought in Israel. One was
the teaching of the great rabbi, Hillel. Moses, in Deuteronomy
24, had said that a man could divorce his wife if he found any
indecency in her. Hillel interpreted that to mean anything
which displeased the husband. If the wife made bad coffee,
he could divorce her. If she did not keep the house clean, if
she got angry or argumentative, or whatever, she could be
divorced. This was the easy school of divorce of that day. Opposed to that was the school of Shammai, another great Hebrew rabbi, who taught that divorce was to be strictly limited,
that only under certain rigidly defined conditions could divorce
ever be granted. So the nation was split between these two
schools of thought.

You will recognize that we have exactly the same problem
today. Perhaps no issue arouses more antagonism or contro-
versy than divorce. What are we to do about divorce? Is it
something rather insignificant, to be taken lightly, that may be

granted because of incompatibility? Or is it something very serious, to be granted only under extremely limited conditions?

In our Lord's answer he develops two very important arguments. He takes them back first to Moses, and discusses divorce as Moses handled it; then, as we will see, he goes back even further—to the time of creation. Let us look first at what he says about Moses:

He answered them, "What did Moses command you?" They said, "Moses allowed a man to write a certificate of divorce, and to put her away." But Jesus said to them, "For your hardness of heart he wrote you this commandment" (Mk. 10:3–5).

Notice that Jesus did not simply answer these Pharisees immediately out of his own authority. He sent them back to Moses first. In other words, he upheld the authority of the Scriptures. Jesus always did. He always referred to the Old Testament as a book that has the answers, as a book that is an authority on life. It is delightful to see that he never superseded that word. He frequently quoted it saying, "It is written . . ." and sent them back to Moses and the law. Even in the Sermon on the Mount he said that he came not to destroy the law but to fulfill it, and he warned against anyone who attempted to destroy the law or change what it said. This is why he sent these Pharisees back to Moses for the answer.

But he did not stop there. He went on to clarify the law. This is what he is doing on this occasion. He is interpreting the word of Moses for them, and revealing to us something that the law itself does not tell us. He is giving us the motive, the reason Moses permitted divorce. Jesus makes a very significant and insightful statement here, one we want to examine very closely. Our Lord goes behind the written statement of Deuteronomy 24, and says, "Moses gave this because of the hardness of your heart." It was because men's hearts were hardened that Moses allowed divorce.

## To Reveal Sin

What does that mean? Well, it is pointing out very clearly that a divorce could occur in order to reveal in public what has been going on in private in that marriage: hardness of heart. This is what the law always does. The law is given to reveal sin. "By the law is the knowledge of sin." So it is perfectly in line with his role as lawgiver that Moses, in giving the laws concerning marriage, should also give permission for divorce in order to make visible what is going on in a family. What was going on in Israel was evidently that hearts were being hardened, and that is why divorce came in.

What is a hardened heart? Well, what would the opposite be? A heart that is softened, mellowed, gentle, and open. There are many occurrences in the Scriptures of the phrase, "hardness of heart." We are warned again and again against hardening our hearts. There is that story in the Old Testament when Moses was sent to Pharaoh and told to deliver the message of God: "Let my people go." When Pharaoh heard that word, he "hardened his heart." That means that he determined to handle it his own way. He determined to respond to the natural inclination of his flesh, to do what he felt like doing in the situation, to handle it himself, and to ignore God. That is hardening of the heart. When you determine that you are going to handle something yourself and not pay any attention to what God reveals about it, you are hardening your heart. This is what was going on in the marriages in Israel.

You can see why. According to Moses, a husband (he looked at it only from the standpoint of the husband) would see some uncleanness in his wife, some indecency. He did not specify what it must be—evidently just something displeasing to the husband, something in his wife that he did not like. And Moses said that because of it, in order to make clear what the husband's attitude was, a divorce was to be permitted. Now, what would this reveal about the husband's attitude? Well, it would be the attitude we all would naturally feel. We all can identify with this because we know how we feel when we find something offensive in someone else. What do we want to do? We want to criticize and complain, even attack, or avoid and reject that person. This is the natural feeling of the heart when we find something offensive in someone else. We object to it, protest it, criticize it, put it down, disparage it in some way—and we reject the person because of it. This is what was going on in these marriages. Husbands were treating their wives with contempt because of something they found in them that they did not like.

What *should* a husband do when he finds something in his wife that he does not like? According to the further revelation of the New Testament in this regard, a husband ought to understand why his wife is like this. This is the word of Peter to husbands: "Husbands, dwell with your wives according to knowledge." That is, do not merely react to them; understand why they are acting the way they are. Dwell with them according to knowledge: give affection to them, honor them, share yourself with them, understand them, restore them, love them. This is what a husband ought to do. This is what a marriage is for—to provide opportunity, as we will soon see, to work out the problem areas, the difficulties, the offensive occasions which arise. But Moses granted divorce, Jesus said, in order to make clear the hardening of hearts that was going on.

What does the softening of the heart involve? A heart is always soft when it recognizes its inability to handle a situation and relies upon the wisdom and power of God. This is what keeps the heart tender, mellow, malleable, reasonable—a recognition of not having what it takes, a reliance upon the wisdom and love of God, and an obedience to him. This keeps the heart tender and soft.

This is what should have been happening in these marriages. But instead, marriages were getting worse and worse. Women were being downgraded and mistreated, treated with contempt and cruelty and harshness. So, in order to make it all clear and visible, Moses granted permission for divorce. It released the women from what may have become almost a hell on earth for them.

It also would tend to open the eyes of the husband. Many people have come to me and said, "I never understood what I was doing to my mate until after the divorce. Somehow this opened my eyes, and I began to see that the problem was with me more than with her (or him)." So many men and women have had their eyes opened because of a divorce. They have learned something about themselves and have gone on to another marriage or to a restoration of the previous one on a quite different basis. That open break made them begin to see themselves for the first time. So this is why Moses granted divorce. It would tend to make public what had been going on in private, so that the world would see the difficulties which were being hidden within the confines of the home.

This is what divorce did then, and this is what it is doing in our own day. We are living in an age when one out of three marriages ends in divorce in this country. That frightening statistic is making people take a different look at marriage. The very fact of the enormous breakdown of the home, which dismays us and marks the deterioration of our society, is also driving us to understand that something else is wrong, that somehow we do not know what we ought to know about marriage. Men do not know how to act as men, and women do not know how to act as women. Something is precipitating such an enormous breakdown that we are forced to look at this problem seriously and earnestly, and there is much healing beginning to take place in our day.

This is what law is all about. It is given to unveil sin and to drive us to grace. Law can never heal the problem; it simply points it out. And the law of Moses, by permitting divorce, simply unfolded a private problem and made it a public predicament, so that everyone became aware of the tendency in this direction. This is why God permitted it. It is perfectly in line with the purposes of law.

## The Real Issue

But our Lord does not stop even there. He now goes on to show us a far deeper and more important matter. Though he has put his finger on the reason marriages fail—because of hardness of heart—he goes on now to show us how they can be cured by revealing to us the purpose of marriage:

> "But from the beginning of creation, 'God made them male and female.' 'For this reason a man shall leave his father and mother and be joined to his wife, and the two shall become one.' So they are no longer two but one. What therefore God has joined together, let not man put asunder" (Mk. 10:6–9).

You recognize those words. They are quoted at every wedding —and yet are singularly disregarded afterward. Jesus goes back now beyond the Pharisees, beyond Moses, beyond the law, beyond the whole Hebrew economy, and takes us right back to the dawn of creation, the very beginning of the human race, and points out to us that what happened there is the determinative factor—not what happened with Moses and the law. The law came in only to show us the problem that existed. The real issue, the real question, is not how to get a divorce; the real question is: how to maintain a marriage? This is what we ought to know.

To answer this question Jesus focuses on three important factors: the actions of God, the desires of God, and the warning of God. First, the actions of God: "From the beginning of creation, 'God made them male and female.' " He made them to be distinct and different sexes. This was no afterthought. The whole creative process, beginning with the very first day of creation, was aimed at that one great fact. God intended to have a race of humans that was divided into two recognizable sexes—male and female. And everything he did from the first verse of Genesis right on through that whole creative sequence until man appeared on the scene was aimed at that one great event. This is how important it was to God. He made them male and female, made them biologically and psychologically different one from the other. This is what he wanted.

Man is a threefold creature, consisting of body, soul, and spirit. In body, men and women are different—visibly and notably, even notoriously different. In the soul, the psyche, they are different as well. This is what the modern feminist movement is denying. It is telling us, in effect, that men and women are no different psychologically. And it is even implying that biologically there is no difference either, that it is only in the matter of child-bearing that there is any difference. This is one of the main weaknesses of this movement. It has corrected a number of abuses, but it is also creating a tremendous number of problems while propounding absurd solutions to these problems. The demand for equality in sports is a case in point. Some leaders in sports are now telling us that if what the feminist movement seems to be insisting upon is actually carried out, it will mean the absolute end of commercial sports as we know them in this country. This is an attempt to disregard the biological differences between men and women, which is absurd.

The so-called "right" of abortion is an example of the end result of this kind of thinking. The proponents claim that a woman has a right to end the life of a baby which started in her womb simply because she does not choose to go on, does not want her body "used" for that purpose. That whole syndrome is a result of this kind of twisted thinking about humanity—ignoring the fact that God made them male and female and that psychologically and biologically men and women are different—and are intended to be. The abolition of what we once called "chivalry," i.e., the courteous attentions

men gave to women, the little recognitions of their need for
protection and shelter and help in various ways, which has
lent so much of beauty and color to life—all of this is being
denied and all but demolished by the women's rights movement. It is all a recognition of the failure to understand this
basic fact that Jesus declares. I would suggest that you read
George Gilder's fine book, *Sexual Suicide,* if you want to see
where this loss of the distinctions between the sexes is taking
us and what harm it is doing already to our society and to all
that God has in mind for humanity. The point Jesus makes is
that God has made the distinctions. They *are* different; men
and women do *not* react in the same way.

But spiritually, men and women are indeed identical. There
is no difference, and therein lies their equality before God. It
is absolutely true that they are equal persons before God and
man. But that is in the spirit. Psychologically and biologically
they are different. When we understand that difference, we
can say, with the French, "Vive la différence!" Thank God
for it! They do not contribute the same things to life and are
not intended to. Men think differently than women; men feel
differently than women. Those differences do not mark an
inequality but a difference in function. That is why men band
together in clubs and unions, whereas women do not. That is
why men are concerned primarily with work, while women are
more concerned with people and relationships. Each respond
instinctively in these ways. Men can be more cold and hard and
offensively objective than women can—usually. This is why
they do not answer questions in the same way. When you ask a
woman a question, usually she will answer according to something she has read into what you asked—either good or bad.
I remember a friend of mine speaking publicly once on the
difference between men and women. He said, "Women take
things more personally than men do." A woman came up to
him at the close of the meeting and said angrily, "I just want
you to know that's not true! I didn't take that personally at

all!" Well, there are differences, and our Lord stresses this fact. God made them male and female. This is what he likes, and this is what makes for richness in humanity.

## Made to Be Joined

We move on from the actions of God to the desires of God: " 'For this reason a man shall leave his father and mother and be joined to his wife, and the two shall become one.' So they are no longer two but one." "For this reason"—what reason? Because they are male and female. That is what they were made male and female for—in order that ultimately they might be joined together and become one. This is what God had in mind in making them male and female in the beginning.

There are a great many implications in this simple statement. First, you recognize that it does away with all such notions as "homosexual marriages." There are no such things— not true marriages. These pathetic misrepresentations in which people of the same sex try to be married are but a poignant commentary upon the twisted, distorted ideas that prevail in society today. It takes a man and a woman to be married. There are no homosexual marriages. And there are no polygamous marriages. You notice Jesus did not say, "God made them male and females," or "males and female." Marriage is one man and one woman, and it always has been, from the very beginning.

But what our Lord makes clear is that this relationship is the highest relationship possible in life. Notice that it takes priority over all others. In the mind and heart of God, the marriage bond is closer even than that of blood relationships. "A man shall leave his father and mother and be joined to his wife." It is a closer relationship than that to any children who follow. People are to become husbands and wives before they become fathers and mothers. This indicates a priority of relationship. A man is closer to his wife, and a wife to her

husband, than they will ever be to their children. Though we
may not feel that way, nevertheless, it is the truth. That is the
way it would ultimately work out best. And, of course, this
prior relationship of husband and wife comes before friend-
ships and all other possible relationships. It is the goal God
had in mind when he made man and woman in the beginning.

What then is the purpose in marriage? It is to become one,
as Jesus said. That is what marriages are for, what they are all
about. Two people, who are disparate, distinct, and different
individuals with different personalities and different gifts, so
blending their lives together that through the process of the
years they become one *flesh*—that is what marriage is. Now,
it is not something that happens instantaneously when you get
married. The wedding service does not make you one. The
first act of sex after marriage does not make you one. It begins
the process, but it does not finish it. It takes the whole marriage
to accomplish this. Marriage is the process of two people becoming one.

Therefore, they are not to live together as roommates.
Marriage is not going your separate ways and having your
separate careers and merely sharing a house and a bed together. Nor are they to split up over every problem or difficulty that arises between them; they are to work them out.
They are not to separate; they are to choose to be together, to
spend the rest of their lives together, in order that they might
merge their lives together. Therefore, they stop being rivals
and start to become partners. A successful marriage is not one
without problems; it is one where the problems are being
worked out, where the husband and wife do not split but
stick together, face up to their problems, discover the hardness
of heart that is there, and learn how God can soften it. In
other words, it is a process, not a single production. It is a
pilgrimage, not a six weeks' performance. It is intended to be
a public portrayal, not a private predicament. It is a life-long

contract, not a renegotiable franchise, as many presume today. So our Lord concludes here with a word of warning:

> "What therefore God has joined together, let not man put asunder." And in the house the disciples asked him again about this matter [his last statement]. And he said to them, "Whoever divorces his wife and marries another, commits adultery against her; and if she divorces her husband and marries another, she commits adultery" (Mk. 10:9–12).

There are some very important principles here. Notice that Jesus lifts the whole matter far beyond the prevailing Jewish view of marriage. The Jewish view, as reflected in the law, was that the initiative was always with the husband. It was only the husband who could divorce his wife. But in our Lord's words here, they are on an equal basis. The man can commit adultery against the wife, and the woman can commit adultery against the husband.

## Creation of an Ecstasy

And he indicates that adultery, sexual infidelity, destroys the work God has been doing in building oneness in a marriage. You see, the phrase, "What God has joined together," does not refer to a wedding service; it refers to what has been going on in the marriage. God has been blending two people —sometimes against their wishes, sometimes with great pain and trouble—but he has been putting their lives together. *He* has been doing it. That is why he has taken them through the trials and conflicts they have gone through. He has been using one against the other to break down their resistance and reveal the hard places in their hearts and to soften them and make them into the people he intended them to be. God has been at work in the marriage. Every couple, when they move into their first apartment or their first home, ought to put up a

sign: "Caution: God at work!" Because that is what he is
doing. He is building a oneness, creating an ecstasy. This is
what marriage is all about—the creation of an ecstasy. It takes
a long time and it involves many steps, but he is producing
something of beauty.

This is why marriage involves sex, and why sex is such an
important part of it. Sex is the visible picture of what a
marriage ought to be. This is why God reserves sex for marriage. What he is really saying (in the beautiful language of
symbolism that God uses with us) is that every marriage ought
to follow the course of the act of sexual union. It ought to begin with some uncertainty, some degree of separation and difference, proceed through a time of increasing relationship and
enjoyment which mounts to a tremendous sense of climax and
of oneness, and concludes at last in a period of restful response
and contentment—and a sense of peace. This is what a marriage ought to be. This is what is pictured for us by every act
of sex in marriage in order that we might understand what God
has in mind. He is building a miracle, he is making a union out
of two, as a picture of what he wants to do for all of humanity.
This is why adultery, sexual infidelity, breaks that work of God
and brings it to an end. God either has to begin it again, or it
ends completely, though perhaps it will begin again in a new
relationship.

I do not intend to impose a sense of condemnation on anyone. But I do want to make clear what Jesus said—that divorce
is sin—no ifs, ands, or buts about it. Divorce is a violation of
God's intention for marriage. It always is, and it always involves some form of sin. But thank God, although that is what
the law says, grace comes in to tell us that sin can be forgiven.
There is the possibility of restoration, of healing, of God's beginning again the work of creating oneness—either with the
same couple, or perhaps if they go on to a different union, each
will have learned lessons which will facilitate the beauty of
relationship that God has in mind.

But I also want to make clear that though there is this way for forgiveness and restoration, we ought to understand that God's way of restoration involves repentance. I have heard Christians say, "If you do not like your present mate, divorce him or her, and get married again. Even if it is wrong, God will forgive you if you ask him to, and you can just go on and enjoy the new union." Well, that bothers me greatly—first, because it takes lightly what God takes very seriously; and second, because it is not true that Scripture teaches that all you need to do is ask God for forgiveness and you are forgiven.

What the Scriptures say is that when you come to the place of *repentance,* you are forgiven. Repentance means the understanding of the awful danger you have put others in, the injury you have caused others and yourself, a sense of shame for that and a willingness to let it come to an end and exist no more in your life, to turn your back on it and walk with God in his forgiveness and restoration into a new life which leads in a new direction. That is repentance, and only then is the forgiveness of God available to us.

This is why Jesus speaks so plainly and yet so graciously in these matters. Adultery does end the marriage, yes; but it does not mean that forgiveness cannot come in and make it over into a new and fresh experience in which God can begin again the work of creating that miracle of oneness which he intends for us. Marriage is God's way of putting two lives together to produce a oneness that will be a testimony to the whole world of the grace and the power of God to change human lives.

# 5

# The Plight of the Overprivileged

This passage in the Gospel of Mark brings before us two familiar stories: Jesus' blessing of the children and the story of the rich young ruler. Although Mark links these two stories together, preachers seldom do. Almost always these are treated in separate messages. But it is very helpful to see how these two incidents tie together and how they will lead us into an understanding, from the lips of Jesus, of what money and riches and the pursuit of wealth will do to us. We start with the story of the blessing of the children:

> And they were bringing children to him, that he might touch them; and the disciples rebuked them. But when Jesus saw it he was indignant, and said to them, "Let the children come to me, do not hinder them; for to such belongs the kingdom of God. Truly, I say to you, whoever does not receive the kingdom of God like a child shall not enter it." And he took them in his arms and blessed them, laying his hands upon them (Mk. 10:13–16).

This passage has been appropriately called the Magna Carta of the children, the Bill of Rights of children everywhere in the world—their right to be appreciated and valued highly. Artists love to paint this scene, and if you have any imagination you can easily picture it—Jesus gathering the children around him, one wriggly little boy on his lap, a little girl standing demurely at his side looking up into his eyes, others clustering around clamoring for his attention. It is a beautiful scene, one which has proven to be a source of tremendous blessing to thousands upon thousands of children around the world, throughout all the centuries past.

## Bumbling Adults

I want to touch on only two major points in this account because I want to tie it with what follows. The first is Jesus' rebuke of the adults in this situation—the disciples. Mark indicates that the disciples were trying to protect Jesus by preventing the parents from bringing their children to him. But when Jesus saw it, he was indignant. In fact, the language is sharper than that in the Greek. He was angry, and severely reprimanded these disciples. He said, "Don't do that; stop it. Let the children come unto me; for to such belongs the kingdom of God." Now, these disciples meant well, as adults often do with regard to children, even though they do the wrong thing. Yet they missed the point of the life of a child. This is what Jesus was correcting. These disciples thought that Jesus needed protection from bothersome children. But what Jesus points out is that the children needed protection from bumbling adults. So he says to the adults, "Stop hindering them, let the children come to me. Get out of their way, and let them come."

This is highly significant because it indicates that children were made for God. This is what Jesus is saying—that he and children were made for each other. You cannot read this without seeing how attractive he must have been to children. They loved him immediately and wanted to come to him. And he indicates here so clearly that it is easy to come to Jesus when you are a child. He is the one they need above anyone else. More than anything else, children need Jesus. This is what he is saying. The one thing adults ought to concern themselves about, with respect to children, is to get out of the way and let them come to Jesus and not to put roadblocks in the path—obstacles arising out of their own selfishness—but to let them come.

The second significant point in this passage is the qualities of childlikeness which Jesus says are absolutely necessary to enter the kingdom of God: "Truly, I say to you, whoever does not receive the kingdom of God like a child shall not enter it." He does not go on to elaborate what these qualities are. He leaves it up to us to discover them as we look at children, for they are something every child represents. Regardless of their background or culture or race or anything else, every child has these qualities. The commentators have had a field day trying to guess what they might be, but Jesus leaves it up to us to try to discover them.

I am a card-carrying grandfather, and lately I have been conducting extensive research into this subject, observing my little grandchildren in an attempt to discover what qualities Jesus has in mind. I want to present to you the findings of this exhaustive (and exhausting) research I have undertaken. The first and most obvious quality about children is that they are simple—not in any derogatory sense—but children are basically uncomplicated, elemental. They go right to the heart of things. This is why children can ask such frank questions. If you pick up a little child in your arms, he is liable to look at you and say, "How come you have such a big nose?" All your adult friends have managed to evade that subject for years, but a child will come right out and ask it. They go right to the point. There is no beating around the bush nor any pretension about them; they are forthright.

This is true in every area of their lives. When their bodily needs are making demands, they must be satisfied. They want to eat when they are hungry. They want to sleep when they are sleepy. They will go to sleep no matter who is around or what is happening. If they want to eliminate, they do so. In the realm of the soul, when they need love, they will come to you and seek affection. They are curious in mind, want to explore whatever is before them, and will go right ahead with it. In the realm of the spirit, they are so expressive of the sense of wonder. I saw a mother dragging a little child down the street one day. The child saw some mica flashing in a stone and stopped to pick it up. "Oh, mother, look! There are stars in the stone!" The mother grabbed her arm and said, "Oh, come on; we haven't time for that." This is the sense of wonder and of mystery in a child, and this is what Jesus meant. A childlike spirit is one which captures this elemental directness.

And a child is wonderfully teachable. Every child wants to learn and is ready to be led. Children recognize their basic need for help and instruction, and they are wide-open, plastic, and easily molded. This is characteristic of children, and this is what Jesus meant. Third, every child is trustful by nature unless you train them otherwise. By nature children are responsive. They respond to what they are taught. They are trustful; they put what they learn into prompt and immediate action. They do not delay or say, "Well, I've got to think this over for awhile," as adults will. If you tell them something, or if they see something, or if they have learned something, they will respond without delay.

These are the characteristics Jesus had in mind. They are essential, he says, to enter the kingdom of God. When you are concerned about your basic needs and listen to the teaching of Jesus and understand what he says about you and about him and respond immediately and wholeheartedly to it, the door to the kingdom of God is wide open to you—not only to enter

it initially but to grow and develop in it and become whole
and strong and healthy. This is what Jesus underscores by
this beautiful picture of the qualities of childlikeness.

So let us move on in the story, as Mark does, to the incident
which immediately follows:

> And as he was setting out on his journey, a man ran up and
> knelt before him, and asked him, "Good Teacher, what must I
> do to inherit eternal life?" And Jesus said to him, "Why do you
> call me good? No one is good but God alone" (Mk. 10:17–18).

This is the incident we usually refer to as "the story of the
rich young ruler," for Luke and Matthew tell us that this
young man was very wealthy and that he was a ruler, an aristocrat. What an amazing picture! This splendid, handsome young
aristocrat coming and kneeling at the feet of this peasant teacher
from Galilee. Notice his opening question: "Good Teacher,
what must I do to inherit eternal life?" It is obvious from this
that the young man had just heard Jesus. He was evidently
present when Jesus answered the Pharisees' question on divorce, and he saw Jesus blessing the children and rebuking
the disciples, telling them they must become like a child to
enter the kingdom of God. Something awakened in this young
man's heart as he listened, and as Jesus starts to leave, he
comes running to him. Kneeling down before him, he says in
effect, "All right, how? How do you enter the kingdom? What
must *I* do to inherit eternal life?"

You cannot read this without seeing that this young man,
whoever he was, possessed at least the first of those qualities
Jesus said you must have in order to enter the kingdom. He
was direct, forthright: he came immediately to the point. His
sense of need was aroused and awakened, and he did not wait;
he came right out and asked, "Lord, what must I do?"

Notice Jesus' reply: "Why do you call me good? No one
is good but God alone." Many have puzzled over why Jesus

said that to this young man. Some of the more liberal commentators have said that this is one clear occasion when Jesus
denies that he is God. Their argument goes like this: Jesus
says, "Why do you call me good? No one is good but God."
In asking "Why do you call me good?" he is, in effect, denying
that he is good: "Don't call me good; I'm not good. Only God
is good, and I'm not God." This is one approach you can take
with regard to these words.

But it is equally valid to take it as a claim to deity on Jesus'
part. What he is really saying to this young man is, "Look,
why do you call me good? What do you mean by 'good'? If
you understand what good means, you will understand that
only God is good. Therefore, if you call me good, you must
understand that you're calling me God." That is an equally
valid interpretation, and it certainly is in line with all the rest
of the claims of Scripture concerning Jesus and his claims
about himself.

So it is apparent that he is probing this young man, searching to see if he is willing to investigate and learn—in other
words, to see if he is teachable or not. He has already demonstrated the quality of elementary and uncomplicated directness.
He came immediately with the question on his heart—came
running, and knelt down before him—his heart open and
seeking. Now Jesus asks, "Are you teachable? Are you willing
to investigate, to think something through?" Then he tests
him on the final quality: "Are you obedient?"

> "You know the commandments: 'Do not kill, Do not commit
> adultery, Do not steal, Do not bear false witness, Do not de-
> fraud [i.e., covet, or steal], Honor your father and mother' "
> (Mk. 10:19).

"What has God said to you? Have you obeyed? Are you
obedient?" This young man's response is beautiful. He says
without hesitation, "Teacher, all these I have observed from
my youth" (Mk. 10:20).

Notice that Jesus does not say to him, "Well, you must be keeping something from me . . . I don't believe that." He does not imply at all that this young man is lying to him, or even deceiving himself in any way. He seems to accept, to be satisfied with, this young man's reply. No wonder Mark goes on to say, "And Jesus looking upon him loved him." Here is an open-hearted, beautiful, moral, excellent young man. Jesus, observing him and hearing his answers, loved him—because he had the qualities which make it possible to enter the kingdom. But he has one thing more to say to him:

> And Jesus looking upon him loved him, and said to him, "You lack one thing; go, sell what you have, and give to the poor, and you will have treasure in heaven; and come, follow me." At that saying his countenance fell, and he went away sorrowful; for he had great possessions (Mk. 10:21-22).

Jesus is saying, "You have the qualities it takes to enter the kingdom. You are simple and direct, you are teachable, and you are obedient. That is, you have been. Now let's see how much you have retained of those qualities. How obedient are you now? How far do you carry this willingness to act upon what you know to be true? You lack but one thing: go and sell all that you have, and give to the poor, and you will have treasure in heaven; and come and follow me."

## Owned By Another God

There is an ironic humor in the young man's response: "He went away sorrowful, for he had great possessions." Would you go away sorrowful if you had great possessions? If you had just won fifty thousand dollars in a television give-away program, would you go away sorrowful? No, you would be rejoicing. But this young man went away sorrowful, *because* he had great possessions. Why? Of course the answer is that he could see there was no way he could serve two masters. Jesus, in that marvelous way of his, had pierced right to the heart of this young man's life, right to the deep things of his spirit, and had shown him that he was owned by another god. This young man, who had everything that money and power and youth could give him, nevertheless, had wanted something far more important. He saw it, caught a glimpse of it, wanted it—eternal life, not just living forever but a quality of life he knew he lacked—an emptiness within his spirit he could not fill. But he knew Jesus could fill it, and he wanted it. He was sorrowful because he also knew from the words of Jesus that he had to give up the other in order to have this; he could not have both. This is why he went away sorrowful—because he had great possessions. Our Lord picks this incident up and goes on to teach some things about affluence in the account which follows:

> And Jesus looked around and said to his disciples, "How hard it will be for those who have riches to enter the kingdom of God!" And the disciples were amazed at his words. But Jesus said to them again, "Children, how hard it is to enter the kingdom of God! It is easier for a camel to go through the eye of a needle than for a rich man to enter the kingdom of God." And they were exceedingly astonished, and said to him, "Then who can be saved?" Jesus looked at them and said, "With men it is impossible, but not with God; for all things are possible with God" (Mk. 10:23–27).

This is a very remarkable statement that Jesus makes. In it he highlights two facts. The first is the terrible danger of affluence, of riches, of seeking to get rich and loving the things money can buy. This, he says, does terrible things to the soul. Most of us, if not openly, then at least secretly, are envious of rich people. We wish we had money. We say so ourselves. And yet, if we really understood what Jesus is saying, we would not feel that way. We would feel sorry for them. We think them overprivileged; Jesus says they are underprivileged. They are deprived people. There is so much they are robbed of by the things they have. So Jesus goes on to point out the terrible danger of affluence. "It is impossible," he says, "for a rich man to enter the kingdom of God."

Let us not minimize his language here. He puts it very bluntly and plainly and uses a very vivid metaphor. He says, "For a rich man to get into the kingdom of God is more difficult than for a camel to crawl through the eye of a needle." I know that some commentators attempt to soften this by explaining that the "eye of a needle" referred to a tiny gate, about four feet high, located in the wall of Jerusalem—by squirming and wriggling a camel could conceivably get through it, and that this is what Jesus is saying here. I do not see much evidence to support that view. I think Jesus meant a literal needle—and you can make it a big darning needle, if you like, with an eye you could put a piece of string through. But try to imagine a huge, lumpy, humpy camel trying to squeeze through a needle's eye and you get the picture Jesus' disciples got. They interpreted him correctly. Jesus is saying to them, "It's impossible." And that is what they thought. They said, "Well, then, who can be saved? What rich man will ever make it, if that is what riches do to you?" And Jesus admitted it. "With men it is impossible . . ."

## Destroyed By Riches

Why is it impossible? What do riches—money, wealth, affluence—do that make it so impossible? It is clear from the context that riches tend to destroy the qualities you must have in order to enter the kingdom of God. They destroy the child-likeness of life—and you can see why. Affluence creates a concern for secondary values. Rich people are not worried about where their next meal is coming from; they worry about what it will taste like and what the setting will be. Rich people are not concerned about whether they will have a roof over their heads and clothing to wear; they are taken up with fashion and style and decor and whether they are in the right mode or not. They are not concerned about whether they worship God rightly or not, but whether they are in a beautiful building which pleases them aesthetically. Riches transfer their concern from the elementary, the necessary things, to the secondary things. This destroys simplicity in life. It is why we have had a revolt of the youth in this country as they have risen to denounce materialism and its emphasis upon other than basic values. Young people have cried out with a loud cry, "Down with the establishment! We don't want it anymore! We want to go back to simple living, to natural ways," because riches destroy simplicity.

Furthermore, affluence destroys teachability. Have you noticed that some wealthy people seem to exercise power which they do not really have in themselves? Stripped of their riches they would appear to be simpletons, almost fools. But because of the power of money and the fact that they can make people jump whenever they want them to, they often are deceived into thinking they are wise and intelligent when they are not at all. Now, some *are* wise and intelligent. I do not mean to put down all rich people. But affluence destroys a teachable spirit because it creates a false sense of power and authority. The man who has power because of his money begins to feel that he ought to be the teacher. He does not need to learn— he already knows everything! This makes for arrogance and indifference and for insensitivity to the needs of others—for isolation and a lack of concern. This is so often characteristic of the wealthy. They may not mean to be this way, but that is what money does. It is a dry rot which eats away at the simplicity of life and at the sensitivity of the heart and removes people from the realities of life.

Finally, affluence gradually enslaves those who are attached to it. It builds an increasing dependence upon comfort, upon "the good life," until people reach a point where they cannot give it up. They are owned by their possessions. As to a habit-forming drug, they become addicted to things, addicted to com-

fort and ease. Therefore, riches destroy the responsive spirit
which is ready and willing to follow truth whenever it is revealed. This is what was happening to this rich young man.
He was almost lost because he was so captured, already in his
youth, by the terrible power of riches. Jesus spoke of this,
calling it "the deceitfulness of riches" which creates illusions
that are not real and makes people think they are something
they are not, so that when truth hits them, they are so bound
and tied to all they own that they cannot get free; they are
helpless slaves.

That is why Jesus said it is impossible—with men. But not
with God. This is the note of grace, and it is the second fact
he highlights. With men it is impossible, but not with God.
God can break that enslavement to riches, and he does, sometimes. A pastor, telling me about his congregation, said, "I
have a number of wealthy people in my congregation, and
they trouble me, because" as he put it, "they dabble with
Christianity." That is often true. I know many wealthy
Christians, and I find that it is rare to find one who is truly
committed to obeying the Word of God. Most go along only
to a point. Thank God there are some who do obey. God has
reached them. I do not know how he does it, but only God
can do it. He can break through, and he does, at times. Sometimes he creates in them a tremendous distaste for things and
makes them so aware of an emptiness and hunger within that
they lose all interest in affairs of business and wealth and
money and, feeling the hollow mockery of it, like this young
man, they begin to search out the realities of life. Sometimes
a man has to suffer catastrophe—almost lose his family or get
sick or have some other disaster occur—before he begins to see
things in their right perspective and comes to Christ in that
way. I could tell you story after story of how God has worked
to open rich men's and women's eyes to bring them back to
the truth and show them the only way that has ever been
provided.

And isn't it interesting that if a rich man does come to

Christ, he must come in exactly the same way as the poorest bum on skid row! He has to acknowledge his complete and utter need and come as a guilty sinner, wretched and miserable and vile, and receive the gift of life at the hands of Jesus from the cross. There is no other way to come—no other way! Rich men have to come that way, too. There is no special way provided for them, except the way that God has made for all.

In contrast to this our Lord now sets forth what happens to those who serve him:

> Peter began to say to him, "Lo, we have left everything and followed you." Jesus said, "Truly, I say to you, there is no one who has left house or brothers or sisters or mother or father or children or lands, for my sake and for the gospel, who will not receive a hundredfold now in this time [i.e., on earth], houses and brothers and sisters and mothers and children and lands, with persecutions, and in the age to come eternal life. But many that are first will be last, and the last first" (Mk. 10:28 31).

The key to this passage is the last sentence: "Many that are first will be last, and the last first." Many have asked, "What is Jesus teaching here? Is he telling us that if we have money and wealth, we must give it all away, as this rich young ruler was instructed? Do we actually have to divest ourselves of our fortune and take a vow of poverty in order to serve Christ?" The passage has been interpreted that way. For hundreds of years in the Christian church, almost from the end of the First Century, men and women have understood it this way. They took a vow of poverty, gave away everything and became monks and nuns and priests and hermits. Some gave up everything and went around as beggars. But did this mean they were truly obedient and fulfilling this passage?

## Whose Money Is It?

"No," Jesus says, "many who are first, apparently, in giving up things, actually turn out to be last." You see, it is not the external things he is talking about here at all. There is plenty

of testimony from the history of the church to the effect that
this cannot be what he means, because these practices often
have not produced even the semblance of spirituality. He is
talking, rather, about the attitude you have toward things. This
is the key—an attitude in which you assume that these things
were given to you not for your benefit alone, not so you can
have a bigger car or a finer home or a place in the country or a
luxurious boat, or whatever. That is not why money is given
to you. It is given to you in order that you might invest it,
employ it to advance the work of the One who gave it to you.
You are a steward of God's affairs, a steward of the things
entrusted to you. And someday every one of us must give an
account of what we used it all for. Now, using it for a certain
degree of your own enjoyment and pleasure is right, too. Paul
says in his first letter to Timothy that God has given us richly
everything to enjoy. But that is not the only purpose of it. It
is also to be used for the advancement of his work.

If you have the attitude that the things God has given you
belong to him and not to you, then if he takes them away, you
do not feel upset; they were not yours to start with! And if he
wants to take them away and use them somewhere else, that
is up to him. This is the attitude Jesus is talking about.

And he says that if you really do have this view of your possessions, you will discover that you can never give up anything
that God does not richly restore to you—in the very terms
which you gave up, only a hundredfold. Now, this is more than
100 percent, as any mathematician can tell you. One hundred
percent would mean that he gave back to you exactly the same
amount you gave up. But this is not what Jesus said. He said
he will give you a hundred*fold*. This means that for every one
thing you give up, he will give you a hundred of them in return. How this is expressed in terms of percentage, I do not
know. I am not that good a mathematician. But how is this
fulfilled? If you are willing to hold things lightly, you will
find that people will open doors to you, other brothers and

sisters will have things that you can use, and you will not have
to pay taxes or rent or anything. You will have homes and
families and boats and pleasure outings offered to you for
God's sake, by God himself, through the friendship and love
of relationships with other Christians. I have found this to be
true.

Of course, Jesus promises persecution, too And he lists it
right in the midst of the passage, making it look like one of
the advantages. And it is, because Jesus is saying that you will
also have the right kind of enemies. During the Watergate
scandal, people regarded it as a compliment to be on Nixon's
"enemies list." They took it as a credit to them that people in
the administration opposed them. Jesus is saying that your
enemies will be the right kind, will be a credit to you. You
will be glad that you have them and that they are persecuting
you because it will be to your honor.

When we understand this, what a difference it makes in our
own life—to hold things lightly for his name's sake and to
understand that God has committed things to us not that we
might please ourselves but that we might advance the cause
he has given us. One of these days, he says, all the fronts and
facades will be stripped away. And many who are last, who
apparently have not given up much at all but who have had
the right attitude about their possessions, will be first of all.
And those who seemingly have given up many things and have
gained a reputation as having sacrificed for the cause of Christ
will be told to take the last seat because they really have not
given up much at all.

I want to close this section by simply giving you Paul's
words in 1 Timothy 6, which really are an exposition of our
Lord's words in Mark:

> As for the rich in this world, charge them not to be haughty, nor
> to set their hopes on uncertain riches but on God who richly
> furnishes us with everything to enjoy. They are to do good, to

be rich in good deeds, liberal and generous, thus laying up for
themselves a good foundation for the future, so that they may
take hold of the life which is life indeed (1 Tim. 6:17–19).

The man who learns how to use money for that purpose has
learned how to be poor in spirit that he might be rich in
stewardship, and thus in life itself.

# 6

# The Ambitious Heart

Our study in the Gospel of Mark now finds Jesus and his disciples on the road to Jerusalem heading for the tense drama of that last action-packed week before the cross. As we read this account, we will see how clearly the Lord Jesus foresaw the cross and all that it would involve and how resolute his determination was to go ahead and face what was coming. We will also see how blind and foolish the disciples were, how stupidly they acted in the face of the revelation which was given to them. And we will see at the end of this passage how Mark illustrates all this with an incident which occurs as Jesus leaves the city of Jericho. Let us begin with verse 32:

And they were on the road, going up to Jerusalem, and Jesus was walking ahead of them; and they were amazed, and those who followed were afraid. And taking the twelve again, he began to tell them what was to happen to him, saying, "Behold, we are going up to Jerusalem; and the Son of man will be delivered to the chief priests and the scribes, and they will condemn him to death, and deliver him to the Gentiles; and they will mock him, and spit upon him, and scourge him, and kill him; and after three days he will rise" (Mk. 10:32–34).

This is the third time we have seen Jesus make this special announcement to his disciples in which he informs them in increasing detail of what the cross will involve. And each time, you notice, he includes the promise of the resurrection, which they never seem to hear. Mark particularly indicates that there is a very tense atmosphere as they are going along the road. He tells us Jesus went first, all alone. Behind him came the band of twelve disciples, who Mark says were astonished, amazed. Behind them came the crowd, the multitude which was following, waiting upon the teaching of Jesus. And they were afraid, Mark says—all of which indicates that there was a strange sense of impending doom, a sense of approaching crisis, with sinister possibilities. The disciples were very much aware of this, and even the crowd felt the tension.

What made the crowd afraid and the disciples amazed, unquestionably, was the attitude of Jesus. One of the other Gospels says at this point that he "set his face like a flint" to go up to Jerusalem. There was a resolute determination on his part to go; he was adamant and would not be dissuaded. Though he was going into danger, and he knew it, and the disciples knew it, and the crowd sensed it, there was this strange, determined resolve on Jesus' part to go forward.

Notice also how filled with detail is the announcement that Jesus makes. He knows what he is heading into. He does not quite know the timing of it, although he knew this would unfold as he went on. But he knew he was going to be delivered into the hands of the priests and the scribes, that he would end up in the hands of the Romans, and would be condemned to death. And he adds three details here which had not been included in any prior announcement: they will mock him and spit upon him and scourge him. How did Jesus know that? He learned it from the Scriptures. Every one of these events is predicted in the prophets. In fact, Luke tells us that at this very point Jesus said to his disciples, "Behold, we are going up to Jerusalem, and everything that is written of the Son of man by the prophets will be accomplished." Our Lord was not given some special insight; he learned it by studying Isaiah 53, Psalm 22, and other Old Testament Scriptures which clearly predict these events.

## Pathway to Glory

So Jesus is on his way to Jerusalem and to the cross, but the disciples, Mark goes on to reveal, see something different awaiting them. They are looking at the pathway to glory:

> And James and John, the sons of Zebedee, came forward to him, and said to him, "Teacher, we want you to do for us whatever we ask of you." And he said to them, "What do you want me to do for you?" And they said to him, "Grant us to sit, one at your right hand and one at your left, in your glory" (Mk. 10:35–37).

Matthew tells us that it was the mother of James and John who asked this of Jesus, suggesting that they had talked her into making this presentation. But Mark goes back of the mother to the two disciples, showing us that it was their idea. Jesus knew the request had come from them, so he answered them. Notice what it is they are asking for, because many have misconstrued this story and felt that these disciples were wrong in asking for this. But that is not true. They were asking for something which Jesus had given them every reason to ask for just a few days before. Matthew records that Jesus had promised them that when he came into his glory they would sit on twelve thrones and judge the twelve tribes of Israel. This is what they have on their minds as they walk up to Jerusalem. There are thrones waiting for them.

So they ask for three specific things: First they ask for *pre-eminence.* They want to sit on those thrones and have the

honor and exaltation that a throne represents. This is what they
had been promised. Second, they want *proximity*. Once the
disciples knew that twelve thrones were waiting for them, as
they had twice now fallen into a discussion as to which of them
would be greatest among them, you can understand why they
would discuss where these thrones would be placed in relationship to Jesus. James and John, talking this over with their
mother, decided there was no good reason why they could
not belong to the inside circle, with one on the right hand and
one on the left. So they come with this request. They want to
be near to Jesus. Now, is that wrong? No, it is not wrong to
want to be near Jesus. They know they are going to sit with
him, and they think it perfectly in order to ask to be given
the positions nearest him. And third, they want *power*. Because, of course, that is what a throne represents. In some
sense, they had already experienced the gift of power from
Jesus. They had been sent out and given power to raise the
dead and heal the sick and cast out demons. So they are only
asking for what had already been promised. There is nothing
wrong with that.

So, when our Lord replies, he does not rebuke them. He does
not say, "What's the matter with you fellows? How can you
be so proud?" He does not rebuff this ambition to be near
him, to have preeminence, and to have power. But he does say
to them, in effect, that they are going about it the wrong way.
This brings us to his answer:

> But Jesus said to them, "You do not know what you are asking.
> Are you able to drink the cup that I drink, or to be baptized
> with the baptism with which I am baptized?" And they said to
> him, "We are able." And Jesus said to them, "The cup that I
> drink you will drink; and with the baptism with which I am
> baptized, you will be baptized; but to sit at my right hand or
> at my left is not mine to grant, but it is for those for whom it
> has been prepared" (Mk. 10:38–40).

He is saying, "The trouble with you fellows is not that you are asking for the wrong thing, but that you are asking for it with no understanding of what is involved. You're ignorant, and know not what you're asking." Then he goes on to tell us what it is they are ignorant of. They are ignorant of the cost of this, the price that it would demand. He implies that he himself is on the same path as they desire to follow. He is on the way to glory. But he is ready to pay the price.

## What Life Hands You

"Are you able to drink the cup that I drink, or to be baptized with the baptism with which I am baptized?" Here he employs two beautiful figures to help us understand what he was facing—a cup and a baptism. What does the cup mean? I am sure most of us have quoted the twenty-third Psalm: "My cup runneth over." What do we mean by that? It has been made into a popular song: "My cup runneth over with love." Well, it is clear that the cup symbolizes the realm of your experience, the circumstances into which you are placed —perhaps producing a joyful, happy reaction on your part. In the Old Testament the figure is also used of things which are not so joyful. Jeremiah speaks of Israel as having to drink the cup of the fury of the Lord—something which was handed to Israel and which they had to drink. So a cup is a figure of what life hands to you, in which you have no choice. It may produce either a good or a bad reaction, but a cup is something given to you which you must drink.

Our Lord, of course, is speaking of the cross. He sees it as a cup given to him by his Father. Later, in the Garden of Gethsemane, he will pray, "If it be possible, let this cup pass from me; nevertheless, not my will but thine be done." So he is speaking of the whole spectrum of events, involving the suffering, the anguish, the pain, the rejection, the mocking, the scourging, the spitting—all of the cross—as the Father's choice for him, handed to him to drink.

When he uses the figure of baptism, what does he mean? Again, this is a figure which is very common in the Scriptures, found in both the Old and the New Testaments. To "baptize" means to "dip," to "place into"—to dip somebody into water or some other liquid, to immerse them in it. The Israelites, as they left Egypt, were "baptized unto Moses in the Red Sea." That is, as they passed through the waters of the Red Sea in the way that was opened up to them, they were surrounded by the waters, baptized by them in that sense. They were overwhelmed by the water. This made them one with Moses. They were identified forever with him by following him into the sea.

This, then, is a figure of some event which was given to the Lord and which would totally affect him. It would overwhelm him. He would be immersed in it so completely that it would touch and affect everything about him. That is a baptism, and that was what was waiting for him. The cross would seek him out at every level of his life, would immerse him and overwhelm him. Remember how beautifully descriptive some of the Psalms are of this idea: "All thy waves and thy billows have gone over me." He would be completely saturated with this terrible event. So he says to James and John, "This is the price of glory. Are you able to pay it?"

Look at the self-confidence they exude. They sound like Muhammad Ali just before a fight! "Sure, Lord; whatever. Just bring it on. We can take it. We are able." Notice how Jesus replies. He does not try to explain it all to them. He leaves it to later events and to the hand of the Father to unfold it to them. Rather, he takes them at their word. "All right. If you want to drink of my cup, and be baptized with my baptism, you shall."

Now, these disciples did not know what they were asking Jesus for. And sometimes neither do we when we ask of God. But God sometimes grants it anyway. If they had known what it meant, they would never have asked for it, I am sure. Dr.

A. B. Bruce, in connection with this, once wrote, "If crosses would leave us alone, we would leave them alone, too." * But they do not. They are handed to us. They are cups given to us. And these disciples could not escape; they, too, would have to suffer like Jesus. They, too, would have to bear reproach and shame and anguish and suffering and death.

As it turned out, this is what happened. James was the very first of the apostles to die, as recorded in the twenty-second chapter of Acts. He was taken and murdered, beheaded, by Herod. John was the last. These two brothers formed a kind of "parenthesis of martyrdom" within which all the apostles in turn were put to death for the sake of Jesus. We are not told exactly how John died, although some of the writings of the early church fathers suggest that he was boiled in oil. Others say that he died a natural death. Though his actual mode of death is uncertain, we do know that he was exiled to the island of Patmos for the testimony of Jesus and underwent much suffering and shame and punishment for the Lord's sake. So Jesus granted them their request.

## Of Men and Glory

Then he went on to explain that he could not grant what else they had asked. "It is not mine to give—but it will be given; somebody will sit there—but it is the Father who determines who it will be." He says something very illuminating here. He does not say, as we might expect, "It is for those who are prepared for it." That is how we would put it. But he says, "It is for those for whom it has been prepared." If you think carefully on those words, you can see that he is implying that the Father chooses men for this honor. He prepares the man for that place by the circumstances, by the cups and baptisms, that he puts him through. And then he prepares the honor for the man. Did you notice that? God always starts with people,

---

* Alexander B. Bruce, *The Training of the Twelve* (Grand Rapids, MI: Kregel Publications, 1971), p. 287.

not with events. His goal is the shaping and molding of lives. That is where he begins. And he fits the events to that end. So, two of them are going to sit at the right hand and the left hand of Jesus. But God is going to mold those two and prepare them for it, and then he will prepare that height of glory for them, as well. At this point Mark turns to the other ten:

> And when the ten heard it, they began to be indignant at James and John. And Jesus called them to him and said to them, "You know that those who are supposed to rule over the Gentiles lord it over them, and their great men exercise authority over them. But it shall not be so among you; but whoever would be great among you must be your servant, and whoever would be first among you must be slave of all. For the Son of man also came not to be served but to serve, and to give his life as a ransom for many" (Mk. 10:41–45).

We have already seen that as they go up the road to Jerusalem, Jesus sees the cross waiting for him; James and John see thrones waiting for them; and what do the other ten see? They see James and John. They are angry and upset at them. Why? Because they got to Jesus first. Obviously, they wanted the same things that James and John did and were angry only because James and John beat them to it. This is often the explanation for our anger, is it not? We are upset only because somebody thought of it before we did.

## No Place for Politics

But notice how Jesus sets aside all this business of politicking and maneuvering and asking for favors and special privileges. That is the way the world works, but it is not to be part of the kingdom of God. In the kingdom—the church, if you like—there is not to be struggling and striving for position and honor. Paul brings this out so beautifully in his development of the body of Christ, in 1 Corinthians 12, where he says that because we have gifts given to us by the Holy Spirit and a ministry opened to us by the Lord Jesus and power granted to us by the heavenly Father, we do not need to be in competition with anybody. Each one has his own ministry, and no one is a rival of any other. We do not need to envy one another. "The eye cannot say to the hand, 'I have no need of you.' " We are not to despise another and look down on him. Nor can the foot say, "Because I am not a hand, I do not belong to the body." All the members are necessary to the body of Christ; therefore, all competition is thus removed from the church.

This is what our Lord wants to set before his disciples, so he gathers them together and patiently—my, how patient he was!—says, "Now, fellows, sit down. I want to say something to you. You've looked at the gentiles, the nonbelievers around. Have you noticed that when they exercise authority, it is always *over* somebody else? They measure their power by how many are *under* them. That is the mark of their authority." Now, I do not think he means to say that must be eliminated or that we should attack that sort of thing. He is simply recognizing it as being there. It is still true today. That is the way people do things, the way they judge their success. And although it produces all kinds of rivalry, competition, skulduggery, politicking, conniving, maneuvering, manipulating, and trying to undercut everybody else, nevertheless, you cannot blame people for that because that is all they know. They do not know any other basis for achieving authority or power.

Notice what Jesus is doing—something very radical. The key is in these words: ". . . but it shall not be so among you." The church is not to be that way. It is not to be set up as a hierarchy of power. There is no chain of command in the church of Jesus Christ. Jesus had already said to these disciples, "One is your Master, and all you are brethren." Every apostle is careful to remind us of the danger of lording it over the brethren, of those in positions of authority thinking they have the right to tell others what to do or how to act or what to think or how to behave, thinking that they have the right to

make decisions which others must follow. This is not true in
the church. Paul is careful to say to the Corinthians, "We are
not lords over your faith." That is, "You can do what you want.
You stand before God, responsible to him not to me." But he
is also faithful to point out what it is they need to do and to
warn them of the results which may follow if they do not want
to do it. But no one is ever to be commanded to do something
by another brother in the church. Only the Lord commands.

We need to think this through in great detail. The church
has always opposed prelacy, i.e., papacy—the idea of a human
head over the entire church. Unfortunately, among Protestant
and evangelical churches we have rejected the idea of one Pope
over all the churches but have placed one Pope in every church.
Surely that is just as bad or worse. No, there is no authority in
being a pastor. A pastor is just a brother who is given certain
gifts in order to be able to help people understand what they
are doing and where they are going. I have no authority over
"my" congregation, nor do they over me. We are all brothers
before the Lord. "It shall not be so among you." The church
must not reflect the position and the practices of the world in
this regard.

Jesus goes on to tell what it is that makes for true authority:
"Whoever would be great among you must be your servant;
and whoever would be first among you must be slave of all."
He has said this before—indeed, here is the theme of Mark's
entire Gospel, but here it is underscored again for us that true
authority arises out of servitude, out of meeting somebody else's
need. Is this not what a servant does? The world is full of
servitude. We are always serving each other and being served
by others. If you check in at a hotel, somebody picks up your
bags and carries them to your room. Of course, you tip him, but
he has served you. The maid comes in and makes up your bed,
cleans up the bathroom, puts new soap in the dishes and clean
towels on the rack. She is serving you. You are paying for it,
I know, but still it is servitude. There are many ways we serve
one another in our homes and various other places. What is

the character of it? It is always meeting another person's need.

This is the key to service. Jesus says that when you are willing to give yourself to meet another person's need, something remarkable happens. Without your even wanting it, necessarily, you establish a strange authority in that person's life. They want to respond. Their attitude toward you changes. They want to do something in return. They do not have to; they want to. It makes them want to respond in some way. This, Jesus said, is a principle in the kingdom of God. This is the way authority arises. Those who have authority are those whom people have learned to respect and honor because they have been served by them—their needs are met by them in one way or another. This is where authority lies within the church. Of course Jesus himself is our great example: "For the Son of man also came not to be served but to serve, and to give his life as a ransom for many." Jesus is the ultimate picture of the servant. The One who had *every right* to authority becomes the One who gives up *everything* to meet our needs. This is the mark of how to function in the kingdom of God.

There is a strange fallacy abroad today that Jesus died in order that we who believe in him might never have to face any kind of death. That is not true. That is not what the Scriptures say or imply in any way. From that comes the idea that when you become Christian, everything ought to smooth out for you and you should have no trouble in your life because Jesus bore it all and you do not have to bear anything. No, the scriptural position is that Jesus died in order that he might go with us through death and bring us out onto the other side. He does not eliminate death at all; it is there. But he goes with us through it and brings us out—this is the point—into a resurrection. That is why he died—to give his life a ransom for many.

## Mark's Illustration

At this point something very remarkable occurs. Suddenly, almost abruptly, Mark changes the subject. He begins to tell of an incident that took place as they were leaving the city of

Jericho. There is no apparent connection with what we have
just been looking at:

> And they came to Jericho; and as he was leaving Jericho with
> his disciples and a great multitude, Bartimaeus, a blind beggar,
> the son of Timaeus, was sitting by the roadside. And when he
> heard that it was Jesus of Nazareth, he began to cry out and
> say, "Jesus, Son of David, have mercy on me!" And many re-
> buked him, telling him to be silent; but he cried out all the
> more, "Son of David, have mercy on me!" And Jesus stopped
> and said, "Call him." And they called the blind man, saying to
> him, "Take heart; rise, he is calling you." And throwing off his
> mantle he sprang up and came to Jesus. And Jesus said to him,
> "What do you want me to do for you?" And the blind man said
> to him, "Master, let me receive my sight." And Jesus said to
> him, "Go your way; your faith has made you well." And im-
> mediately he received his sight and followed him on the way
> (Mk. 10:46–52).

It looks at first glance as though there is no connection. But
was it just by chance that as Jesus was leaving Jericho, a blind
man named Bartimaeus was sitting by the road? Well, it can
be read as though all that Mark is doing is giving a chronicle
of the events that happened, and this was just one of those
events which occurred by chance as they left the city. But do
things happen that way? Or was it perhaps by the prearrange-
ment of an infinitely wise Father—a Sovereign God—who arranged to have a blind man named Bartimaeus there because
it tied in directly with what Jesus had been saying and exactly
illustrated something more he wanted the disciples to know?

Let me show you some rather interesting ties in this little
account with what has gone before. First of all, you notice that
there is an unusual repetition in mentioning the name of this
man. We are told that Bartimaeus, a blind beggar, the son of
Timaeus, was sitting by the roadside. The name "Bartimaeus"
means "son of Timaeus." So it is really redundant to say

"Bartimaeus, the son of Timaeus," because they mean the same thing. So, in a sense, this name is being underscored for us as is no other name in the account. There must be something about this name that Mark wants us to note. When you look up the Greek meaning of "Timaeus," you discover why. The word means, "honor." This beggar was named "the son of honor." Now, what was it that James and John had asked Jesus for? Honor, was it not? ". . . that we may sit, one at your right hand and one at your left, in your glory." Here was a blind man, named "the son of honor," who sat beside the road.

Notice, too, that Mark skips over a number of events. He eliminates the things that we know happened in Jericho from the other accounts. He says, "And they came to Jericho," and then he skips over the story of Zacchaeus and all that happened in connection with this short man whom Jesus met and went to lunch with, and he goes directly to the time when they left the city in order to emphasize the tie with what has just gone before.

Furthermore, you notice that when the blind man came to Jesus, Jesus asked him, in verse 51, "What do you want me to do for you?" When James and John came to Jesus with their request for honor, in verse 36, he asked them, "What do you want me to do for you?" Exactly the same words! What was the trouble with these disciples? They were blind, were they not? They could not see what was involved. They wanted something, but they did not see what was connected with it. They could not see the cup, the baptism, the hurt, the cross. They were blind. What was the matter with Bartimaeus? He was blind. Jesus asked, in both cases, "What do you want me to do for you?"

## The Son-of-Honor's Request

So the point of the story, the truly impressive thing about this account and the reason Mark has placed it here, is what Bartimaeus did. Here was a man who was conscious of his

blindness, whereas the disciples were not. When he heard that
Jesus of Nazareth was passing by, he became tremendously
excited and began to demand his attention. "Jesus, Son of
David, have mercy on me!" Everybody said, "Shh! We're trying to hear what he's saying!" Bartimaeus paid no attention,
and said again, "JESUS, SON OF DAVID, STOP! HAVE MERCY
ON ME!" They shushed him again: "Many rebuked him, telling him to be silent," but he would not be put off. Finally, he
got Jesus' attention. And when our Lord stopped to serve this
man, to meet his needs, he called him to himself and asked
him, "What do you want me to do for you?"

Doesn't that seem a silly question to ask a blind man—
when you have the power to restore his sight and he knows it?
But Jesus asked him this question. And Bartimaeus put it
so simply, "Lord, I want to see. Let me receive my sight."
And immediately Jesus said, "It is done. Your faith has made
you well." And Bartimaeus could see for the first time in his
life.

So why do you think Mark has put this account in this particular place? Well, Jesus is saying to his disciples and to us,
"When you come asking for good things from God, ask also to
be able to see what they involve. Ask to have your sight given
to you so that you see yourself and all that may be needed before God can answer that prayer."

There is a verse in Proverbs that says, "The spirit of man is
the candle of the Lord, searching the hidden things of the
heart" (Prov. 20:27). In contemplating that verse one time
there came flooding upon me a consciousness of my own life,
and I remembered that when I was just a young Christian, I
felt that God had only a few minor things to change about me
and then I'd be pretty nearly perfect. I knew there *were* some
things that needed to be changed—I could see them—but they
were not too serious. And once those were changed, there
would not be much left that God had to worry about. That
was many years ago, but "the spirit of man is the candle of the

Lord, searching the heart." In the hands of the Holy Spirit my human spirit was used of God to begin to unfold to me, gradually, over the years, all the many areas in which there were deeper involvements in evil than I ever dreamed. And I remember how, through the years, there came painful experiences—cups and baptisms that I had to go through—which opened my eyes until I began to see with increasing clarity how much of my life has been possessed with a spirit of selfishness, how I have injured others and hurt those close to me, and how much I was in the grip of evil forces in my life which controlled and devastated me. And yet, along with every new revelation of the depths of my own vileness, there also came a revelation of the cleansing power of God. Through the course of the years, I discovered that as my self-esteem began to sink lower and lower, my sense of self-worth began to rise higher and higher. I understood that I had value only as God possessed and cleansed my life. This is why I could sing, as so many of us have sung, about amazing grace and thank God for having saved such a wretch as I. I began to pray increasingly, as the years went on, the prayer that David prays in Psalm 139: "Search me, O God, and know my heart! Try me and know my thoughts! And see if there be any wicked way in me, and lead me in the way everlasting!"

I think this is what God wants us all to pray. This is what Jesus wanted his disciples to pray. How blind they were! How foolish and ignorant and self-confident they were, not knowing what was in them and what God would have to do to remove it before they could receive what they asked for.

# 7

# The King Is Coming

A beautiful song which has been written in these last few years—one of many marvelous compositions which have come out of the great spiritual movement of our day—is called, "The King Is Coming." Perhaps you have heard it. I have seen entire audiences greatly moved as that song was sung. It would be very fitting music for the study we come to now because this is the story of Jesus' "triumphal entry" into Jerusalem, when the whole city became aware that the King was coming:

And when they drew near to Jerusalem to Bethphage and Bethany, at the Mount of Olives, he sent two of his disciples, and said to them, "Go into the village opposite you, and immediately as you enter it you will find a colt tied, on which no one has ever sat; untie it and bring it. If any one says to you, 'Why are you doing this?' say, 'The Lord has need of it and will send it back here immediately.' " And they went away, and found a colt tied at the door out in the open street; and they untied it. And those who stood there said to them, "What are you doing, untying the colt?" And they told them what Jesus had said; and they let them go (Mk. 11:1–6).

94

It is very apparent from this brief account that Jesus had made certain prearrangements for this day. He knew that he was coming into the city and that he was to fulfill prophecies which had been made hundreds of years earlier. So he had made arrangements in advance for fulfillment of the prophecy concerning this colt. Thus, we do not need to see this as some miraculous supply of his need. The colt was tied where it was because he had arranged for it to be there. When the word was given that the Lord had need of it, this was all the owners required because the Lord Jesus had made such arrangements earlier. He had made a quick trip to Jerusalem about three months before, in what would be our month of January, and it is very likely that he made these arrangements at that time. For Jesus knew the day and the hour he was coming into Jerusalem, and he knew what would be required of that moment. In the book of Zechariah, in chapter 9, this event is described clearly. The prophet had cried out, "Rejoice greatly, O daughter of Zion! Shout aloud, O daughter of Jerusalem! Lo, your king comes to you; triumphant and victorious is he, humble and riding on an ass, on a colt the foal of an ass" (Zech. 9:9).

Jesus knew that prophecy, knew that it would need to be fulfilled. So he had made arrangements, I think, that on this particular day he would be coming into the city on a colt. He knew exactly what day this would be, for the book of Daniel tells us that almost five hundred years earlier an angel had appeared to the prophet Daniel and had told him that a certain amount of time had been marked out by God and would be given over to the fulfillment of certain climactic and dramatic events which concerned the people of Israel. And the time when this was to begin was clearly given. It would be when the Persian king, Artaxerxes, issued an edict for the rebuilding of the walls of Jerusalem. You will find that edict recorded in chapter 2 of the book of Nehemiah. And when this heathen king issued the edict, he unknowingly set in motion God's clock for the Jewish nation. Daniel was told that four hundred and

ninety years must run their course before all of God's events
would be fulfilled, and the passage of four hundred and eighty-
three of those years would be marked off by the arrival in
Jerusalem of Messiah the Prince.

Many years ago there was a brilliant lawyer who served for
a long time as the director of England's famed Scotland Yard.
His name was Sir Robert Anderson. He was also an avid and
devout Bible student. Sir Robert Anderson, with his precise
mind and his training in logic, analyzed the book of Daniel
and determined the exact date when that decree of Artaxerxes
was issued: March 28, 445 B.C. Counting from that date and
making the necessary corrections for calendric errors, he determined that on April 6, A.D. 32, Jesus rode into Jerusalem—
exactly four hundred eighty-three years later.

Now, if a man in the Nineteenth Century could take these
Scriptures and figure out the very date on which this event took
place, surely the Son of God, who also had the book of Daniel
and knew it very well and was taught and illuminated by the
Holy Spirit as he read its pages, would know the day that he
was to come into Jerusalem. So he made the arrangements to
enter the city and came riding down the slopes of the Mount of
Olives on a donkey, on a colt on which no one had ever sat, in
fulfillment of the predictions of Zechariah and Daniel.

I find it interesting that all three of the Synoptic Gospels
tell us that this was an animal on which no one had ever sat
—a young donkey. When I was a boy in Montana, some of us
high school boys would try to break horses for amusement.
Some of the full-grown ones were a little too much for us to
handle, so we concentrated on the yearling colts on which no
one had ever sat. I can give you firsthand testimony that these
animals do not welcome that experience! And even though
they are just one year old, they are quite capable of dumping
you along the wayside. Here is an animal that no one had ever
sat on—but Jesus sat on him, and the colt was quiet, responsive,
obedient, and carried him through the streets of the city.

## The Very Words of David

"Well," you say, "if Jesus arranged all this and worked it all out, doesn't that mean that this is really not a fulfillment of prophecy at all?" Well, I think it is true that he arranged some of it, but he did not arrange all of it. There were things he could not have arranged: the response of the crowd as he came into the city, the attitude of the rulers—these were far beyond his control. Yet when Jesus came riding down the slopes of the Mount of Olives, the crowd welcomed him and greeted him just as the prophets of old had said they would do:

> And they brought the colt to Jesus, and threw their garments on it; and he sat upon it. And many spread their garments on the road, and others spread leafy branches which they had cut from the fields. And those who went before and those who followed cried out, "Hosanna! Blessed is he who comes in the name of the Lord! Blessed is the kingdom of our father David that is coming! Hosanna in the highest!" (Mk. 11:7–10).

From other accounts we know they were not so much citizens of Jerusalem as people from Galilee who were in Jerusalem for the Passover feast. Many were children. And yet, as they saw Jesus coming, they felt deeply moved to cry out the very words that fulfilled Psalm 118. You cannot read this account without seeing that these words must have been much in the Lord's mind as he went through this experience—and, unaccountably, also in the minds and hearts of these people. In this Psalm David cries, "The stone which the builders rejected has become the chief corner stone. . . . This is the day which the Lord has made; we will rejoice and be glad in it. . . . Blessed is he who comes in the name of the Lord." Those were the very words that these people cried out, as Jesus rode through the streets.

Luke adds something very interesting in his account of this event:

And when he drew near and saw the city he wept over it, saying,
"Would that even today you knew the things that make for
peace! [Notice his phraseology: "even *today*," i.e., "even *this
day*."] But now they are hid from your eyes. For the days shall
come upon you, when your enemies will cast up a bank about
you and surround you, and hem you in on every side, and dash
you to the ground, you and your children within you, and they
will not leave one stone upon another in you; because you did
not know the time of your visitation" (Lk. 19:41–44).

Amazing words, fulfilled to the letter forty years later when the
Roman general Titus brought his armies and began a prolonged siege of Jerusalem—and eventually overcame it. Against
the general's command the temple was burned, and the gold
of the temple's treasury ran into the cracks of the stones. In
their efforts to get at the gold the soldiers pried apart the
stones and, literally, left not one stone standing upon another.
As he rode down the mountain, Jesus knew all that was coming and he wept because, as Luke records him saying, "You did
not know the time of your visitation."

That is one of the most tragic sentences in the Bible. God
had sent out invitations to this great event five hundred years
before—had told when it would happen, had given an exact
time schedule, and had told how to recognize the King. But
when he came, nobody in the city knew who he was except a
passel of Galilean peasants and their children who were there
celebrating the Passover. What an ironic twist! Yet that is
often what happens with us. We do not know the time when
God is suddenly in our midst.

## Official Tour of Inspection

In Mark 11:11 we read the purpose of our Lord's visit:
"And he entered Jerusalem, and went into the temple; and
when he had looked round at everything, as it was already late,
he went out to Bethany with the twelve."

That does not sound very significant, yet it tells us what he came to do. This was an official visit of the King of Israel, an inspection tour of the heart of the nation. He went into the temple, where the very heartbeat of the nation was throbbing in the worship that was lifted up to God. And he looked at *everything.* We know what he saw: commercialism, money-changers, exploitation, corruption, and injustice. He saw dirt, filth, and squalor, pride, hypocrisy, and haughtiness. He saw that religious ceremonies were being carried on without any meaning whatsoever. But he did not say a word. He just looked around at everything. Nobody noticed him because he had been there many times before. But they did not know this was an official tour of inspection by the King.

God comes into our lives that way, doesn't he? Wouldn't it be wonderful if God looked at us only when we come to church on Sunday morning, if he would read our hearts only when we are sitting with the Word of God open before us and when we're thinking all the nice things we should? But he does not; he catches us in the bedroom and in the kitchen and at the office—and in our car! He comes in and looks around at everything and does not say a word.

## Poor Innocent Fig Tree?

In verses 21 and following we get the results of this inspection. Jesus did not say a word when he looked around, but the next day, before he returned to the temple, he took a symbolic action.

> On the following day, when they came from Bethany, he was hungry. And seeing in the distance a fig tree in leaf, he went to see if he could find anything on it. When he came to it, he found nothing but leaves, for it was not the season for figs. And he said to it, "May no one ever eat fruit from you again." And his disciples heard it (Mk. 11:12–14).

As we will read shortly, the disciples were surprised the next day when they saw that the tree was withered clear to its roots.

Many have been amazed at this miracle. It seems so unlike Jesus. It is the only miracle in the entire record of Jesus' ministry which is a pronunciation of judgment and condemnation and destruction upon anything. It seems so strange that it would occur to a tree that did not have figs when it was not the season for figs. This has bothered many people. Why did Jesus curse this tree that did not have figs when it should not have had any?

I want to tell you that I puzzled over this problem for years until I finally decided to conduct some research. When I moved to California, I planted a fig tree—just to see what it would do and to learn from it. I learned the answer to this riddle from the fig tree in my yard. The first spring I watched with interest as the barren limbs of that tree began to swell, the buds began to fill out, and the leaves began to appear. And to my astonishment—I did not know this about a fig tree—little tiny figs appeared right along with the leaves. I thought, "Well, that's strange: the fruit comes right along with the leaf. Fig trees must be very unusual that way." So I watched these little figs grow and turn from green to yellow, beginning to look as if they were ripe. One day I sampled one. To my amazement, instead of being full of juice and pulp as a normal fig would be, it was dry and withered inside, with no juice at all. I opened another and found the same thing. I thought my fig tree was a lemon!

But then, to my amazement, I saw that the tree began to bear other figs, and these began to swell and grow bigger. And when I opened one, I saw that it was a normal fig, rich and juicy and filled with pulp. And the tree has borne a great crop of figs ever since. So I learned something: a fig tree has two kinds of figs—one that I call "pre-figs," which look like figs but are not, but which always appear first. I learned that if a tree does not have those pre-figs, it will not have real figs later on.

## Like Fig Tree—Like Nation

This is the explanation for what Jesus found. It was not the season for real figs. But when Jesus looked at this tree, he found no pre-figs either, so he knew that this tree would never have figs; it would produce nothing but leaves. The life of the tree had been spent producing its luxuriant foliage—it looked like a healthy tree, but was not. And so he cursed it, and the next day it was withered to its very roots. That tree was a symbol of the nation Israel, as we will see, because what follows is a dramatic acting out of the symbol of that cursed fig tree:

> And they came to Jerusalem. And he entered the temple and began to drive out those who sold and those who bought in the temple, and he overturned the tables of the money-changers and the seats of those who sold pigeons; and he would not allow any one to carry anything through the temple. And he taught, and said to them, "Is it not written, 'My house shall be called a house of prayer for all the nations'? But you have made it a den of robbers" (Mk. 11:15–17).

Jesus took two very significant actions here which are tantamount to the cursing of this nation, just as he cursed the fig tree when he found it with nothing but leaves. The first is that he cleansed it from all the false manifestations which had crept in. He cleaned out the commercialism of this temple—for the second time. According to John's Gospel, three years before at the very beginning of his ministry, he had entered this temple and had swept out the money-changers in very similar fashion. Now he does it again, and he refuses to allow anyone to commercialize these sacrificial offerings. They were selling animals as a "service" to the people. And because they would accept only the official temple currency, money-changers set up shop (another "service") where people could exchange normal currency into temple currency. The money-changers and traders

were making an excessive profit at this business, and Jesus
swept the whole mess out.

But then he did something even more significant. Mark says,
"He would not allow any one to carry anything through the
temple." If you refer to the books of Leviticus and Numbers,
you see that God had instituted a certain set of rituals for the
temple which necessitated that the priests would carry many
things through it. They had to bring the animals into the
temple, bind them upon the altar, and slay them. They had to
catch the blood of these animals and carry it in basins into the
holy place to sprinkle it on the altar of incense. They had to
take the bodies of the sacrifices after they were burned and
carry them back out again. So there was a continual procession
of priests through that temple all day long, carrying out the
system of rituals which God himself had given this nation. But
on this day, when Jesus came into the temple, he stopped it
dead in its tracks. "He would not permit any one to carry anything through the temple," which means that, as the authorized
King of this nation, he rejected its worship and refused to
acknowledge it as of any value any longer. Though the Jews
later restored this traffic and kept it up for forty years more
until the temple was destroyed, never again did those sacrifices
have any meaning before God. This represented the cursing
of the heart of the nation because it had nothing but leaves.
It appeared to have life, but in reality did not. It appeared to
offer hope to men and women of the nations of earth. From all
over the earth people were coming to the temple at Jerusalem,
hoping to find an answer to the emptiness and the burden of
their heart but finding no help there at all. So Jesus cursed the
nation.

The immediate result was the withering of the life of the
nation. It is manifest in these words: "And the chief priests
and scribes heard it and sought a way to destroy him." They
had never done that before. Every earlier account of the op-
position to Jesus of the chief priests and scribes cited their get-

ting together to discuss what they ought to do with him. Now the matter is settled. Now they intend to destroy him, and they need only discuss how to go about it:

> And the chief priests and the scribes heard it and sought a way to destroy him; for they feared him, because all the multitude was astonished at his teaching. And when evening came they went out of the city (Mk. 11:18–19).

That was the point of no return for this nation. It was undoubtedly this act of Jesus—stopping the worship in the temple —which resulted in his death within the week. The scribes and the Pharisees would no longer put up with anything Jesus did or said from that moment on. This sealed his death, but it also sealed their destiny. They thought they were getting rid of him. But it was he, as the King in all his majesty, who had pronounced sentence upon them and had sealed their doom.

## No Faith, No Life

The next day, coming back into the city, Jesus begins to explain some of these strange things. And here all that has happened in these tremendous events is borne home to our own hearts:

> As they passed by in the morning, they saw the fig tree withered away to its roots. And Peter remembered and said to him, "Master, look! the fig tree which you cursed has withered." And Jesus answered them, "Have faith in God" (Mk. 11:20–22).

Does that answer not strike you as strange? Many have read this passage and, neglecting to read it in its context, have taken this to be a kind of formula Jesus is giving us which would enable us to work miracles. But if you read this in connection with all the events of this passage, where it belongs, you will see it is not that. He is not telling us the secret of how to curse fig trees; he is telling us the secret of how to live so as not to

be cursed. This nation was cursed because it had lost faith in
God. It had substituted instead an empty procedure, a meaningless ritual, a performance only, which had an outwardly religious glaze to it but inwardly was unreal and hypocritical.
They had lost faith in God, and so the life of God which was
in them was dried up and withered.

This is what Jesus is telling us: "Have faith in God," means
that this is the way to live! This is the way to have life full and
rich and meaningful—to trust that the living God knows what
he is doing, to believe what he says, to obey what he commands, and to open our life to him so that he may enrich us
and flow through us and make us a fruitful person or a fruitful
nation, as the case may be. "Have faith in God." This is the
answer. A nation or an individual which begins to dry up this
source of life, whose faith becomes dull and dead, is in danger
ultimately of losing the capacity to have life within him. That
is what this nation did. Then Jesus went on to say something
even more puzzling:

"Truly, I say to you, whoever says to this mountain, 'Be taken
up and cast into the sea,' and does not doubt in his heart, but
believes that what he says will come to pass, it will be done for
him" (Mk. 11:23).

Once again, we extract that out of context and read it as a
magic formula for doing amazing things. Imagine going around
and commanding mountains to lift themselves up and cast
themselves into the sea! We say, "The secret is, you've got to
believe that the thing is going to happen." That is like telling
someone not to think of pink elephants. If you tell somebody,
"You can have all the riches of the world given to you if, when
you ask for them, you will not think of pink elephants," do you
know what will happen? They will never get the riches, because under those circumstances it is impossible to stop thinking of pink elephants!

## Pride Is the Mountain

But Jesus is not giving us a formula here for throwing
mountains into the sea. He is telling us that to have faith in
God at times is difficult to do. He knows that. There are mountains which oppose our faith and make it difficult for us. There
are obstacles to faith. This nation had experienced those obstacles, and they were formidable. One was their slavery under
the Romans. Another was the apparent silence of God. All the
many circumstances which aroused doubt and fear in their lives
were like a mountain which opposed the great fact that they
were to have faith in God. Jesus says, "I tell you, if you ask in
faith, that mountain will be removed." And then he goes on to
tell us how:

> "Therefore I tell you, whatever you ask in prayer, believe that
> you will receive it, and you will. And whenever you stand pray-
> ing, forgive, it you have anything against any one; so that your
> Father also who is in heaven may forgive you your trespasses"
> (Mk. 11:24–25).

Now, do not remove that verse from its context! Jesus is
saying, "The great hindrance to having faith in God is pride,
the pride which refuses to forgive. That is like a mountain
which fills up your whole life. All you can see is that big mountain looming before you—that is blocking the life of God in
your life. You have the power to have that removed if, when
you stand and pray, you will forgive those who have offended
you." The only thing that stops us from forgiving one another
is pride. We feel justified in wanting others to forgive us, but
we also feel justified in believing that we have to exact a price
for the hurt they have caused us. So, in many ways—subtle,
or direct and open—we insist that we will not forgive, that they
have to pay for what they have done to us. We are going to be
avenged! We are going to have our revenge for what has hap-

pened. Somehow, we are going to make them crawl, make
them beg or plead for forgiveness. "And that," Jesus says, "is
a great mountain which needs to be removed, for it is blocking the flow of the life of God to your faith. So when you stand
and pray, life will flow from God when you are able to recognize that you, too, need forgiveness. God has forgiven you. Like
the very person you are holding a grudge against, you need
forgiveness also. God has offered it freely to you; give it just
as freely to them."

You know, after thirty years of ministry, I can recite evidence by the yard that this is true. The one thing above all else
which seems to block the flow of the life of God to an individual, to a church, or to a nation is this unwillingness to forgive, this holding of grudges, this desire to put somebody down
in order to feel good oneself, this unwillingness to set these
things aside and let God heal all the hurts of life.

That is why Jesus puts his finger on this one thing. The nation of Israel lost its life because it would not forgive the gentiles, the Romans, who had offended and grieved it. Instead,
it gathered its robes of self-righteousness about it and looked
with pride up to God and said, "I thank God I am not like
these other people." God says that is what ends the life of a
nation. That is what ends the life of a church. And that is what
ends the spiritual life of an individual, cutting him off from
God.

May God help us, then, to forgive one another. This is no
option, nor is it a luxury; it is a necessity of life. The ground
of our own forgiveness is that Another has paid the price, Another has assumed our debt, Another has borne the hurt, so
that we can be free. We can have all his love, and all his life
—freely, without doing anything on our part to merit it. How
much more then should we extend that same mercy and love
to all who have offended us and forgive them, so that the life
of God may flourish in our midst, and we may grow strong
together in Jesus Christ our Lord.

# 8

# By What Authority

In our study of our Lord's visit to Jerusalem—that last, climactic, and fatal week of his life—we see the Lord in confrontation with various authorities of the area. He is dealing with the central issue of all time, the basic question of everyone's life: What is the final authority of life? Should I obey the state, or should I obey my conscience? Which is higher, the church, or the secular government? Should I walk by reason or by faith? Should I follow science or religion? These are questions every one of us must face, and we are helped greatly by the words of our Lord in this account.

Remember that Jesus, after cleansing the temple for the second time, then stopped the offerings and sacrifices of the Mosaic system. That was a very dangerous and daring thing for Jesus to do, and everyone was shocked and stunned by his action. These sacrifices were the heart and center of the life of the nation. Yet here was Jesus, on his own authority, bringing this priestly traffic to a halt. This would be equivalent to Billy Graham walking up to the pulpit of the First Baptist Church of Dallas, Texas, and ripping apart the King James Version

of the Bible. Blasphemy! Everyone would be stunned by such
an action.

Now Mark records the reaction that follows:

> And they came again to Jerusalem. And as he was walking in
> the temple, the chief priests and the scribes and the elders came
> to him, and they said to him, "By what authority are you doing
> these things, or who gave you this authority to do them?" (Mk.
> 11:27–28).

You can sense the bluntness and the sternness in their voices.
Now the fat's in the fire for sure. There will be no more fun
and games; the issues are right down to bare bedrock. They
know it, and Jesus knows it. So they come to him with the
ultimate question, "Who gave you the authority to do this?
Who told you that you could act like this?" That question is
behind all human behavior. When you refine any issue down
to its essentials, what you have left is the whole issue of authority in life. Why do you act the way you do? How do you
justify what you say and do? No man ever is his own ultimate
authority. We all refer to something other than ourselves—
something that compels us or something we feel is important
—that governs our decisions. When we deal with this question
of authority, therefore, we are dealing with what is absolutely
basic and fundamental to all human behavior.

These were no second-rate individuals who came to Jesus.
This was a very imposing delegation made up of Caiaphas the
high priest, Annas, his father-in-law (who was regarded as
virtual high priest), the scribes—the body of men who interpreted the law of Moses—and the elders who were officially
appointed to serve in the Sanhedrin, the ruling body of the nation. This was an august council—the Jewish heads of state,
under the overarching rule of Rome—who came to Jesus with
this question.

## Jews in a Jam

In the answer Jesus gave to these men, we have one of the most amazing accounts in Scripture. What our Lord does in this moment of pressure is very revealing. The first thing he does, with utter calmness, is to examine *their* credentials. Then, he predicts their ultimate downfall. In verse 29 of chapter 11, we see him examining their credentials: "Jesus said to them, 'I will ask you a question; answer me, and I will tell you by what authority I do these things. Was the baptism of John from heaven or from men? Answer me.' " Notice the directness of that word; he puts them right on the spot.

> And they argued with one another, "If we say, 'From heaven,' he will say, 'Why then did you not believe him?' But shall we say, 'From men'?"—they were afraid of the people, for all held that John was a real prophet. So they answered Jesus, "We do not know." And Jesus said to them, "Neither will I tell you by what authority I do these things" (Mk. 11:31–33).

I love that answer! But notice that the Lord seized upon a most remarkable test. He asked about the *baptism* of John, not the ministry of John. Nor did he ask about John himself. He asked, "Was the baptism of John from heaven or from men?" You see, the baptism of John was something different, something new and startling that had never occurred before. The priests, of course, had had many washings, connected with their duties under the levitical system, but this was always done in the temple according to a prescribed ritual. John, however, was different; he was not a priest, yet he baptized. He did it in the rivers and streams—wherever he could find enough water. Because it was something quite new, John's baptism would immediately arouse the question, "By what authority do you give us a new ritual in Israel?" So Jesus seizes upon that and says to these men, "What do you think of this innovation of John's? Was it from God or from men?" Notice again how he simplifies the issue, clearing away all nonessentials. All authority is either of God or men; there are no other authorities. We are either trying to please God and obey him, being responsive to truth that he reveals and responsible to his power, or we are trying to please men, to manipulate them and use them, or to gain something from them.

Now it is clear from their answer that they knew he had them in a dilemma. In chess you call this a "fork," where, no matter what you do, you are going to lose a piece. These men knew that whatever they said, they were trapped. If they said, "It was from God," the Lord had them. He would say, "Why then didn't you accept him?" And if they said, "It was from men," they knew the multitude standing around them would be very displeased, and they dared not say that either. So they copped out and said, "We don't know." So Jesus said, "All right; I won't tell you either." But he did not leave them there; he went on to expose their utter dishonesty. By their answer they revealed that they really did not care whether John's baptism was from God or not. They were not interested in the truth, nor were they willing to answer that question at all; they only cared about serving their own interests. Thus they revealed themselves as being opposed to God's authority, acting only out of the intrigues and craftiness of men.

## Isaiah's Parable

Now our Lord proceeds to make that fact visible to everybody by telling a story. He takes the attack, and predicts their ultimate downfall:

And he began to speak to them in parables. "A man planted a vineyard, and set a hedge around it, and dug a pit for the wine press, and built a tower, and let it out to tenants, and went into another country" (Mk. 12:1).

Now the scribes and Pharisees and chief priests would immediately recognize that story. Jesus is borrowing almost the exact words of Isaiah, chapter 5, where the nation is described as a vineyard. God had dug a pit and built a tower to protect his vineyard and had come looking for fruit. These Jewish leaders would immediately recognize that this was about them. Jesus goes on,

> "When the time came, he sent a servant to the tenants, to get from them some of the fruit of the vineyard. And they took him and beat him, and sent him away empty-handed. Again he sent to them another servant, and they wounded him in the head, and treated him shamefully. And he sent another, and him they killed; and so with many others, some they beat and some they killed. He had still one other, a beloved son; finally he sent him to them, saying, 'They will respect my son.' But those tenants said to one another, 'This is the heir; come, let us kill him, and the inheritance will be ours.' And they took him and killed him, and cast him out of the vineyard" (Mk. 12:2–8).

Can you imagine the boldness and daring of our Lord who in this veiled and yet very clear way threw this parable right into their teeth! He is describing to them who they are and what they are doing. And indirectly, he is answering their question, "By what authority do you do these things?" He says, "Here is my authority: I am the owner of the vineyard. I am the rightful heir to it. I am the beloved Son whom the Father has sent. You've killed the prophets, stoned and beaten those who came from God; now here I am, the Son." And he told these men what they would do: They would beat him, kill him, and cast him out of the vineyard. Jesus is under no delusions as to what is going to happen to him. But then he goes on to predict what would ultimately happen, that God has the final answer. He asks, "What will the owner of the vineyard do? He will come and destroy the tenants, and give the vineyards to others" (vs. 9).

In Mark's account it looks as though Jesus answers his own question, but Matthew makes it clear that Jesus asks the question, and it is the scribes and the chief priests who give the answer. Jesus tells the story, and says, "Now, in that story, what would the owner of the vineyard do?" Matthew records that the scribes and chief priests said, "Why, he'll come and destroy the tenants, and give the vineyard to someone else." Jesus says, "You are right. You have judged yourselves. Have you never read the scripture:

> 'The very stone which the builders rejected has become the head of the corner; this was the Lord's doing, and it is marvelous in our eyes'?" And they tried to arrest him, but feared the multitude, for they perceived that he had told the parable against them; so they left him and went away (Mk. 12:10–12).

Theirs is a false religious authority that presumes to dictate and to usurp power and authority that was never rightfully theirs. Jesus makes this crystal clear. But he says, "That is not the end. When human authorities act that way, you can remember that God is not yet through." What he said here actually took place. On the day of resurrection, the one whom the builders rejected indeed became the foundation of the building. As the resurrected Lord he stood with his disciples and said, "All power, *all* power in heaven and on earth has been given unto me." He is the Lord of everything, in control of history, the ultimate determiner of all that happens in human affairs. Forty years later, Roman armies came in, surrounded the city of Jerusalem and captured it, and the chief priests, the scribes, and the elders were led away in chains into captivity to be dispersed among the nations. God did exactly what he said he would do in this parable.

This is a lesson to us and to all who read this account—man's authority is always limited and can never be equated with God's rule and authority in the affairs of men. Men's

authority is always limited as to duration. Men can sit on the
seat of unrighteous, unjust power for just so long, and then
something happens to sweep them out of office. J. B. Phillips
said, "Remember that the powers-that-be will soon be the
powers-that-have-been." The prophet Ezekiel had said that
God's process throughout history is declared in these words,
"I will overturn, overturn, overturn, till he shall come whose
right it is to reign." No evil power can remain in control very
long. God's hand is at work in history to overthrow and to re-
place one power with another. Man's power, therefore, is always limited in duration.

## To Pay or Not to Pay

In the next account we have our Lord's encounter with another form of human authority:

> And they [the chief priests and scribes] sent to him some of the
> Pharisees and some of the Herodians, to entrap him in his talk.
> And they came and said to him, "Teacher, we know that you are
> true, and care for no man; for you do not regard the position of
> men, but truly teach the way of God" (Mk. 12:13–14).

What oily scoundrels these were, coming with such pious-
sounding words! Yet this group was made up of two parties
who hated each others' guts. The Pharisees and the Herodians
were political enemies who got together only because they were
both confronted with the threat of Jesus to their vested interests. They came to Jesus with a question all worked out: "Is
it lawful to pay taxes to Caesar, or not? Should we pay them,
or should we not?" (vs. 15).

We still ask ourselves this question. Should you pay taxes to
a power that uses them wrongly? Is it right to pay your good,
hard-earned money to a government that wastes it or puts it
to a purpose that you adamantly oppose? Should you, or should
you not? That is a great moral question.

But knowing their hypocrisy, he said to them, "Why put me to the test? Bring me a coin, and let me look at it." And they brought one. And he said to them, "Whose likeness and inscription is this?" They said to him, "Caesar's." Jesus said to them, "Render to Caesar the things that are Caesar's, and to God the things that are God's." And they were amazed at him (Mk. 12:15–17).

I remember reading some time ago of a brilliant young lawyer who had been raised a pagan and had no use for Christianity. Someone had given him the New Testament, and he was reading it through. When he came to this account in Mark, he read this question with great interest, for he himself had recently been involved with just such a dilemma. He said he could hardly read fast enough to see what Jesus would have to say. When the full impact of the actions of Jesus hit this man, he was utterly astonished. He dropped the Bible and said to himself, "That's the most amazing wisdom!" For our Lord did not try to answer the question directly. In that wonderful way he had, he called for a coin—he had to borrow one, for he had none of his own—and held it up. "Whose picture is on this coin?" he asked. They said, "Caesar's." He said, "All right, then it must be Caesar's money. Render to Caesar the things that are Caesar's. But God has got his stamp upon you, so render to God the things that are God's."

He shows us clearly that human authority is not only limited in duration; it is limited in its scope. It deals with only a part of man. The secular government is ordained of God. The apostle Paul tells us that plainly, and Peter says the same thing: "Be subject for the Lord's sake to every human institution, whether it be to the emperor as supreme, or to governors as sent by him . . ." (1 Pet. 2:13–14). Jesus himself acknowledges, as does all of Scripture, that God is behind secular government—even bad government. For the emperor that Peter referred to was none other than Nero, wretched moral degenerate that he was. Yet Peter says, "Honor the emperor."

But human government, Jesus says, has only limited control over men. It has certain powers over the bodies and minds of men. It can regulate our conduct to some degree and has the right to influence and regulate our attitudes and actions, what we say, and how we say it. But there is one area in human life over which secular power has no control, and that is the human spirit. Secular power cannot legislate as to whom we worship, who governs our conscience, and who constitutes the ultimate authority of life. "Render to Caesar the things that are Caesar's." Certain things do properly belong to Caesar; give them to him. But other things about you belong only to God, so give those to God.

Great wrong is done by secular might when it tries to govern and control the worship of men. Viciousness and exploitation always result when a secular power seeks to invade that proscribed area of human existence, the human spirit. That is what the American revolution was all about. The record of history is filled with the resistance of men to any invasion of that area of life from secular sources. Jesus is saying that the ultimate issues of life belong to God, not to man, and human authority is, therefore, limited in its scope.

## A Clearly Ridiculous Question

Now in the last incident in this passage he is confronted with still another form of human authority, what we call "rationalism," or the scientific mind, the authority or power of the thinking of men—and this is very much with us yet:

And Sadducees came to him, who say there is no resurrection; and they asked him a question, saying, "Teacher, Moses wrote for us that if a man's brother dies and leaves a wife, but leaves no child, the man must take the wife, and raise up children for his brother. There were seven brothers; the first took a wife, and when he died left no children, and the second took her, and died, leaving no children, and the third likewise; and the seven left no children. Last of all the woman also died [worn out]. In the resurrection whose wife will she be? For the seven had her as wife" (Mk. 12:18–23).

This is an utterly ridiculous, mocking question. Mark makes this very clear, for he tells us right at the beginning that these Sadducees were rationalists, materialists—humanists, we would call them. They did not believe in the supernatural. They did not believe in angels or spirits or that anything invisible had reality. They did not believe in a life after death, nor in a resurrection, as Mark clearly states. And yet they come with the question, "What's going to happen in the resurrection?"

You can see the sneering contempt that is behind this question. It is an absurd, contrived story, concocted just to try to trap Jesus. It never really happened, and I doubt if it could happen. It is simply a ridiculous story that they made up. I am sure Jesus must have been tempted to treat it as such. He could have asked them why they did not investigate her cooking, for example. When a woman has seven husbands one after the other, all of whom die off, something is suspicious in the kitchen! But he does not. Notice how he answers them:

> Jesus said to them, "Is not this why you are wrong, that you know neither the scriptures nor the power of God? For when they rise from the dead, they neither marry nor are given in marriage, but are like angels in heaven. And as for the dead being raised, have you not read in the book of Moses, in the passage about the bush, how God said to him, 'I am the God of Abraham, and the God of Isaac, and the God of Jacob'? He is not God of the dead, but of the living; you are quite wrong" (Mk. 12:24–27).

Now he is very blunt and minces no words. "You are wrong," he says. "Your whole view of life has made you wrong. You're so sure you're right. You have narrowed life down to a very limited view, and you say that's all there is. And looking at life from that narrow perspective, you cannot see the reality that lies beyond. You're wrong because you fail to recognize two great facts: One, God has knowledge that man does not have. God's knowledge is infinitely greater than man's. That is why we have the Scriptures. You don't know the Scriptures, obviously, for that is where God's knowledge, far greater than man's, is made known to us." Things that only God knows are made known to us in only one place, the Scriptures. The folly of men who reject the Scriptures is that they thus lock themselves into a narrow slice of life, bounded only by that which can be seen and felt and weighed and measured and verified by the senses of man. Man himself then becomes the boundary of life.

Second, Jesus said, "You don't know the power of God. Even if you do know the Scriptures, you don't believe them, because you don't believe that God has power to do what man cannot do. You've bounded your life by the knowledge of man and the power of man. You've exalted man to the place where you think he knows everything that can be known, and there is nothing beyond his power. So, you're wrong." I remember reading this passage many years ago, as a young Christian, and I was intrigued by Jesus' words: "You are wrong for two reasons. You know neither the Scriptures nor the power of God." And through all the years since I have been checking this out. No matter in what area it is found—business, science, religion, politics, family life—every error of life can be attributed to one of those two things. Either you do not know the Scriptures, or you do not know the power of God. You do not know what a living God can do and what a living God knows; that is why you are wrong. This is the fatal weakness of what we call "the scientific mind."

Now, within the purview of its field science is very helpful and does some tremendously helpful things. I am not speaking against science, but we must always recognize what Blaise Pascal put so beautifully when he said, "The ultimate purpose of reason is to bring us to the place where we see that there is a limit to reason." That is what is wrong with the so-called scientific mind. These men were excluding all the supernatural from their thinking. Scientists often do this, saying, "In the scientific realm there is no room for speculation about life after death. Nobody can prove it or verify it; nobody who has been there has ever come back. Therefore, it is an irrelevant fact that has no meaning to life."

## Limited in Dimension

But Jesus says, "You're wrong. And the reason you are wrong is that you do not see reality." Though it is true that as a scientist, such themes as life after death and the resurrection have nothing to do with your examination of the here and now, what you do not see is that you are more than a scientist, you're a person. And as a person, you cannot escape that problem. You must some day confront the reality of your own death. If you shove that off into the background and never examine it, never look at it, you're going to find that—as a person, because you are the way God made you—you will be haunted with fears that you will never resolve and troubled with guilt that you cannot handle. And because of these fears and guilts, your thinking and attitudes will become distorted, and you will make wrong decisions. Even your scientific judgment will be colored and distorted by these things. As a scientist, you end up wrong, because as a person, you refuse to recognize the facts about your life. That is what is wrong with science as an ultimate authority. So our Lord is clearly telling us that human authority is limited in its duration, limited in its scope—for it deals with only a part of man—and it is limited in its dimensions. It deals only with time and not with eternity.

In contrast to this, God's authority rings through this passage as being worthy of man's responsible obedience. For God's authority, in contrast with man's, encompasses all of time. It never changes. It is never one thing during one age and something else in another. It is not subject to the laws of dynasty and rule; it is never overthrown. It is exactly today what it was in the days of Abraham, Isaac, and Moses. God's authority and power govern the whole of man. It touches our body, soul, and spirit, and all that we are is responsible before him. God's authority reaches beyond time through all the limitless ages of eternity, beyond the visible into the realm of the invisible. It touches the great realities that constantly bear upon our lives that cannot be seen by eyes or felt by hand or weighed by human instruments. As men, therefore, we stand in the presence of a God who is sovereign over every part of our lives.

This is why Jesus on another occasion said, "Don't fear men. Don't fear those who can kill the body and that's as far as they can go. But rather, fear him who is able to cast both body and soul into hell." It is not that he wants us to see God as a terrible and severe judge; it is as a loving, sovereign Father that he wants to redeem us. He wants us to recognize that nothing men do can overrule what God can do, for men cannot overthrow God. Human authority must always be ruled by and be subject to the overarching authority of God. And when we live in terms of that reality, all else will ultimately find its place in the picture of life.

# 9

# Top Priority

Certain times of the year bring out something of the pressure and the complexity of life. Sometimes life can get so full and busy that you wonder how in the world you can ever handle it all. Where to begin? What do you do first? And where do you go from there? We will get great help from Jesus' words found in the twelfth chapter of Mark.

Jesus has been confronted by the scribes, chief priests, Pharisees, Herodians, and the Sadducees as they have tried to trap him in his words. And now, in the midst of that great discourse, he takes the attack and begins to speak about things of very great import to us:

And one of the scribes came up and heard them disputing with one another, and seeing that he answered them well, asked him, "Which commandment is the first of all?" Jesus answered, "The first is, 'Hear, O Israel: The Lord our God, the Lord is one; and you shall love the Lord your God with all your heart, and with all your soul, and with all your mind, and with all your strength.' The second is this, 'You shall love your neighbor as

yourself.' There is no other commandment greater than these"
(Mk. 12:28–31).


In the answer our Lord gives to this insightful scribe's question, you have his listing of the priorities of life. Number one is to begin with God. When you are troubled, when you do not know what to do first, when you feel you do not have enough resources to handle something or are puzzled and bewildered, start with God and love him.

When we think about our own lives, we have to admit that we seldom start with loving God. Almost always we start with the demands made upon us instead of looking to the God who will lead us through the puzzle, the problem and the pressures that confront us. We are so wrapped up with the problem that we can't get our minds off it and onto God. He says to start with loving God. When you start with God, you start with one who sees the whole problem, not just a part of it, but the whole problem and everything involved in it. Our trouble is that when we start with our own situation, we are so limited that we do not see it in the right perspective. So we are to start with God's thinking, with God himself.

## He Started It

But God himself does not begin there. There is something that precedes our love of God that our Lord takes for granted. What is that first thing? It is that God approaches us first. The command from Moses in Deuteronomy 6 that Jesus quotes here is a command that man is to love God. But that love is not possible until we have begun to see that God has loved us first. Our love, therefore, is the response of man to God. If all we were faced with was a demand for love from a God up there somewhere, we would find it difficult to respond. He would appear to be our enemy or our judge or even our executioner. But the Scriptures never really start with our response.

Do you remember how John put it in his letter in 1 John 4:19, "We love, because he first loved us."

Man's responsibility is to respond to God's love, which is reaching out to us on every side—reaching out in nature, reaching out in the supply of all that is being given to us day by day. We are never to forget that the things we enjoy—the food, the air, the sunshine, the shelter, all these material things of life that we need—come from the hand of God. It is God who gives them. It is God's goodness protecting us, sheltering us, and watching over us that keeps us from being ravished and destroyed by the forces that are at work for evil in our lives. God's sheltering hand is protecting us. So when you think about the love of God, especially the love that redeems us, the proper and only response of the heart is to love God back with all your heart, soul, mind, and strength.

Now notice that Jesus tells us the process by which we are to love God. You see, love is not just a momentary feeling; it is a logical and specific action. If loving God is the key to life, the central truth of our humanity, how do we do it? Jesus quotes Moses as indicating certain processes by which this happens. The order given in the verse proceeds from the heart through the soul and mind to the whole man, the strength. This is reversed in our experience. In experience we begin with the mind. Truth comes to us from observation. We see things, we feel things, we hear things, we read things about God, we observe the record of our lives, the experience around us, and truth hits us first in the mind. That is why Jesus said that we are to love the Lord our God with all our minds and think about what God is doing for us and through us and to us in our lives.

Next, the truth lays hold of the emotions or the soul, as it is listed here. Love the Lord your God with all your soul—that is the quality of your emotional response. Truth hits the mind and then it moves to the emotions and grips them and you begin to feel moved by the truth your mind comprehends.

The third step is to assault and lay hold of the will—the heart, it is called here. The word "heart" is used in several ways in the Scriptures. Sometimes it refers to the will, sometimes to the emotions, but here it is the will that is in view. We are to choose with the heart, choose with the will—"For man believes with the heart and so is justified," the Apostle tells us in Romans 10.

Once our will (heart) is moved, then the whole man is involved. We love God with all our strength; which means we obey what he says.

How do you love God? Observe the truth, allow it to touch the emotions, then to challenge and move the will, and, finally, to engage the body. We are to do this again and again and again. You start solving problems by responding to God's love in this way. Only then can you love your neighbor as yourself. That is putting things in the proper priority.

## Singing Response

Now before we depart from the first commandment I want you to notice something. This progression of our love of God is beautifully portrayed for us in some of the hymns that we sing. When we sing hymns, we are worshiping God, and in many cases these hymns reflect the order in which we respond to God's love. One of my favorite hymns is Charles Wesley's great song, "And Can It Be." You remember how it begins:

> And can it be that I should gain
> An interest in the Saviour's blood?
> Died He for me, who caused His pain?
> For me, who Him to death pursued?

What is this hymn saying? It is challenging the mind about this amazing record of the Son of God. God himself in human flesh came to die and suffer on my behalf that I might have a part in all the great working of his universe, might be involved with him and linked with him and all that he does. That truth staggers the intellect. The mind is called on to think about Christ's work and to consider these questions. Then the heart responds; the soul, the emotions, come in.

> Amazing love! How can it be
> That Thou, my God, shouldst die for me?

The following verses repeat the process of contemplating various aspects of the death of Christ on our behalf and then inviting the heart to respond again. In the fourth verse the will is called into play:

> Long my imprisoned spirit lay
> Fast bound in sin and nature's night.

You see, the process is to look back over the past and think it through. Then God works.

> Thine eye diffused a quickening ray
> I woke, the dungeon flamed with light.

Here is God at work in a darkened heart. Then the writer continues:

> My chains fell off, my heart was free.

There is the freeing of the will to act. My heart—the very term that Jesus used in the verse in Mark, my heart, my will—was free.

> I rose, went forth, and followed thee.

Finally the body is brought in; the whole man must follow God. This is loving God with all the heart and soul and mind and strength together.

We are to solve our problems by responding again and again to God's love. When we start with God's love, we are ready to turn to our particular problem—our relationship to our wife, children, neighbor, friend, or boss. Then we are freed to love our neighbor as ourselves. We are now to pass on to somebody else the same process that reached us and won a response from us. We can show them the same love that we ourselves have received. Our response to God's love makes it possible. If we start with our neighbor, we get so wrapped up with all the hurts, difficulties, and friction that we start responding in the same way they treat us. But when we start with God and have experienced his love and responded to it with love, then we can pass it along to our neighbor. It never works when we start with "love your neighbor" first, as we always are trying to do. All the social humanities of our day teach us that we ought to love our neighbor, and they are right. But if we start there, without loving God first, we find ourselves incapable of loving others.

Not long ago a young man came to me and told me how uptight, angry, and hostile his sister was towards their whole family and how offended he had become at her attitude. He had responded to her with the same hostility. They got into an argument; they had threatened each other. It was the usual story that we all are so familiar with. I put my arm around him and said, "You know, I remember about five years ago a certain young man coming to church with the most hateful look on his face that I think I have ever seen. He was hostile and angry and upset. He would scowl and snarl at everyone who tried to talk with him. He went around with a constant frown and nobody could get him to do anything. But you know, I have been watching that young man through the years and he has been changing. I see a smile coming to his face. I see a friendly grin for everyone now, and a different attitude—a wholly different outlook, an eagerness to help, and a cheerful spirit." And I asked, "What do you think has made that change?" I knew that he knew that I was talking about him. He hung his head for a moment. I said, "You didn't change because people treated you the same way you treated them, did you? It was love that changed you. Somebody loved you in spite of the way you acted. Somebody reached out to you, showed interest in you, encouraged you, and hugged you. That is what made the change, was it not?" He stood there for a moment with his head down, and then he said, "Yeah, I guess that is what she needs." He went home determined, I knew, to respond to his sister with love.

Love is not just a word to write on a plaque and put on your wall. Love is what you do to people that irritate you when you are upset and angry and hostile and feel like striking back. You start with God. Remember his love to you. Remember his forgiving spirit, how he wipes out everything without requiring anything from you. Respond to it and pass it on immediately to the one you are involved with. Love toward God is the most important thing in our lives; it is top priority. Everything else will flow from that love, but if you put anything else first, the whole process will soon break down.

God knows that we need love, and to fill this need he sets us in families where we start out life being loved and babied. Love is poured into us, and we begin to see and learn what love is and how much we need it. And for awhile those around us fill all our love needs. But we find out sooner or later that the cistern runs dry—people are not an adequate source of love. They never were intended to be. If you keep depending upon people for love, you will find their love has limits; it can only go so far, and it cannot meet your needs.

The whole purpose of life is to lead us to the final and ultimate truth that God is the one who loves us and can fully satisfy us. God's love meets the deepest needs of our life. I find that Christians resist that truth. They do not want to believe that. They do not even want to take love from God because they are so insistent that it come from people. But when you try to meet your love needs with people, you find out that those needs cannot be fully met, and you feel lonely. You can be with people who are trying to love you with all their hearts, and yet be lonely. Love-needs are met only by God himself, and that is why we have to start with God.

## Not Far from the Kingdom

Jesus goes on to point out something further:

> And the scribe said to him, "You are right, Teacher; you have truly said that he is one, and there is no other but he; and to love him with all the heart, and with all the understanding, and with all the strength, and to love one's neighbor as oneself, is much more than all whole burnt offerings and sacrifices" (Mk. 12:32–33).

This scribe, unknown and unnamed, saw a great truth. He saw that God is not at all interested in the performances of our life; he is not interested in mere religious activity. But these things point to something that God is interested in. And this man had seen it. "And when Jesus saw that he answered wisely, he said to him, 'You are not far from the kingdom of God.' And after that no one dared to ask him any question" (vs. 34).

Our Lord commends this scribe, but he points out that he is still not laying hold of the kingdom of God. He is close. He is seeing truth that is very important—that God is concerned about the inner attitude and not the outward performance of life—but the scribe still doesn't grasp the whole truth. He is still not able, in other words, to love the Lord his God with all his heart and all his soul and all his mind and all his strength. He is missing something.

And now our Lord goes on to say what it is. I am sorry that in our English text the connection between these two paragraphs is lost. But in the Greek text it is very clear that the two are linked together. It says, "Jesus answered as he taught in the temple." Jesus "answered." Answered what? He answered the question that would be in the scribe's heart: "You say that I

am very close to the kingdom of God. What more is necessary?" Jesus answered by putting a question to these scribes:

> "How can the scribes say that the Christ is the son of David?
> David himself, inspired by the Holy Spirit, declared, 'The Lord
> said to my Lord, Sit at my right hand, Till I put thy enemies
> under thy feet.' David himself calls him Lord; so how is he his
> son?" And the great throng heard him gladly (Mk. 12:35–37).

Now according to Mark's record no one answered that
question. But our Lord is thrusting deeply now and is driving
home a very important point to these scribes. When David
says, "The Lord (i.e. Jehovah) said to my Lord, sit at my right
hand," he is calling the Messiah "my Lord." Now all these
scribes would have agreed with that. Jesus' question is: How
can the Messiah be David's Lord and still be his son? The
answer, of course, is the mystery of his own person. He is
descended from David according to the flesh, but he is the
Lord of Glory according to the Spirit.

Jesus' identity is the central issue of life. As Paul tells us,
the whole of creation is moving toward that final day when
that question will be thoroughly and completely answered,
when at last the whole record of human war and conflict and
evil is ended. Then God will have finished his amazing and
remarkable workings through human life and history. It will
culminate in that great scene in which God has highly exalted
Jesus and given him the name which is above every name, that
at the name of Jesus, every knee shall bow, every tongue con-
fess that Jesus Christ is Lord to the glory of God the Father.
Jesus is the issue. His lordship is the key. That is why all
through Paul's epistles you find many practical exhortations
which are linked always with "as unto the Lord": "Wives, be
subject unto your husbands as unto the Lord." "Husbands love
your wives as Christ loved the church." "Children obey your

parents in the Lord." "Stop stealing for the Lord's sake." "Masters be kind to your employees for the Lord's sake." Everywhere, Jesus Christ as Lord is the governor of life.

Is that the way you are living? Does Jesus govern all that you say and all that you do? Jesus is the issue. His lordship is what releases the kingdom of God in our life. All the greatness and glory of God come pouring into us when he is Lord. Paul writes to the Colossians and says, "Whatsoever you do in word or deed, do all in the name of the Lord Jesus and to the glory of God the Father."

## Two Copper Coins

Mark concludes this account with a contrast that indicates how Jesus' lordship will manifest itself. The true expression of a heart submitted to the lordship of Jesus is demonstrated by the contrast between a pompous, proud, religious scribe and a humble, poor, and godly widow.

> And in his teaching he said, "Beware of the scribes, who like to go about in long robes, and to have salutations in the market places and the best seats in the synagogues and the places of honor at feasts, who devour widows' houses and for a pretense make long prayers. They will receive the greater condemnation" (Mk. 12:38–40).

That is the false expression of godliness. It is possible, we all know, to pretend to be godly. In some way or another we all succumb to this temptation, do we not? We love the places of honor. We love the salutations in the marketplaces. We love to make long and impressive prayers for others to hear. If it is not these specific pretenses we use, it is the modern equivalents of them. We love to impress people by our godly talk, by our knowledge of the Scripture, by our attendance at church, by various and sundry religious performances, and we want others to know about these things. But in contrast:

And he sat down opposite the treasury, and watched the multitude putting money into the treasury. Many rich people put in large sums. And a poor widow came, and put in two copper coins, which make a penny. And he called his disciples to him, and said to them, "Truly, I say to you, this poor widow has put in more than all those who are contributing to the treasury. For they all contributed out of their abundance; but she out of her poverty has put in everything she had, her whole living" (Mk. 12:41–44).

The religious performance among these scribes and Pharisees had reached such an absurd state of affairs, Josephus tells us, that some of the Pharisees, before they made their contribution to the great collection box Jesus was watching here, actually summoned a trumpeter to go before them to get everybody's attention. Then the Pharisee would come up and proudly deposit a bag of gold in the treasury chest. He wanted everybody to see his ample gift.

In some ways we do the same thing. I heard about a dear man who stood up in a meeting where they were taking an offering and subscriptions of money and said, "I want to give $100—anonymously." But Jesus said the one who really moved his heart and contributed tremendously to the kingdom of God was a little, unnamed, unknown widow who had no influence, who had no outward posture of being worth anything. She came and put in two tiny coins that added up to no more than a penny; but she gave it because she loved the Lord her God with all her heart, all her soul, all her strength, and all her mind. And Jesus said, "She has done more for the kingdom of heaven than all the outward performances of all these others combined."

What is that saying to us? We are so intent upon the fact that God wants some kind of activity on our part, are we not? We think that the way to serve God is to do spectacular or showy things—to win a lot of people to Christ, or to give our time, or work in open ways. Yet the Scriptures tell us over and over that works are just the channel. God wants performance, but only if the attitude of our heart is right. If you cannot do anything outwardly, your attitude may still be right—toward your neighbor, friends, children, husband, wife, your boss, and those who irritate you. If your attitude is one of love, love received from the God who loves you, then you are advancing the kingdom of God far more than all that is done outwardly by the greatest saints of our day and time. Is that not amazing! God says, "You can serve me in the quiet of your home and by the gentle, sweet spirit that you display in the midst of pressures and problems. You have done more to advance the kingdom of God than those who get out and proclaim the word on public address systems everywhere." That is the way God sees life.

Now that is both discouraging and encouraging. It is discouraging for those of us who have a public ministry. We are mentally jotting down in the back of our minds how impressed God ought to be with our performance. But God is looking at the heart. This is very encouraging for us to remember in those private moments when our attitude changes. Nobody was watching, nobody saw what we were thinking, yet, instead of being sharp and caustic and sarcastic, we were sweet and patient and gentle. God says the kingdom of God is advanced by that event, by that activity, by that attitude. These words of Jesus really search our hearts, do they not? And yet how wise and true they are as he puts his finger on the thing that really counts.

# 10

# Watch

Now we come to the great prophecy of Jesus which deals with the last days of the planet Earth just before the return of its King in power and glory. This passage is familiarly called the Olivet Discourse because Jesus gave this great message as he was seated on the Mount of Olives. Looking out over the city of Jerusalem, just a day or two before his crucifixion, he was contemplating the fate of the city in response to questions his disciples asked him. We have those questions in the opening verses of chapter 13:

And as he came out of the temple, one of his disciples said to him, "Look, Teacher, what wonderful stones and what wonderful buildings!" And Jesus said to him, "Do you see these great buildings? There will not be left here one stone upon another, that will not be thrown down." And as he sat on the Mount of Olives opposite the temple, Peter and James and John and Andrew asked him privately, "Tell us, when will this be, and what will be the sign when these things are all to be accomplished?" (Mk. 13:1–4).

This account makes clear that the disciples must have been rather upset by the actions of Jesus during that last week. He had cleansed the temple and had severely scolded and condemned the leaders of the temple. The disciples evidently feel that he has been too harsh, and they are trying to woo from him some positive statement about the temple. So they indicate to him the greatness of the temple buildings and the stones of which they were made. Josephus tells us that some of these stones were forty feet long and eighteen feet high—truly massive stones. But Jesus' answer again disturbs and perplexes them, because he said that these stones, as great as they were, would be cast down, and the temple would be destroyed. The disciples were troubled by this, and they selected a delegation to go and talk it over with Jesus. They chose the two pair of brothers, Peter and Andrew, and James and John, who were in the inner circle. Finding Jesus seated on the mountainside, they asked him privately, "When will these things be, and what will be the sign when they are to be accomplished?"

This is the question almost everyone wants to ask when they read this prophetic section: "When is this going to happen?" We are familiar with these words in which Jesus foretells what will be happening on earth before his return. But the question which has seized the minds of men has always been, "When is it going to happen? Will it be in my lifetime? And what will be the signs so we'll know when it will begin to happen?" For twenty centuries men have been asking this question. For twenty centuries men have been anticipating that the coming was to be in their own time. We must honestly face this. Every generation has thought Jesus was coming back within their own time because of signs which they saw, or thought they saw, in the immediate events of their day.

## The Wrong Question

But I think it clear, as you read this account through, that to ask "When?" is to ask the wrong question. Jesus makes clear that if you focus on "When?" you are going to be misled and ultimately deceived. And this has been the record of what has happened to many people—many leaders and teachers—as they have tried to dig out the answer to the question, "When?" Jesus does not ignore this question, but he leaves it to the end.

We will go through this whole chapter now and survey what he actually does say and how he handles this question when he comes to the end. There are four sections of Jesus' message which relate to the question of the disciples, "What will be the sign when these things are all to be accomplished?" And there is one section at the end where he deals with the question, "When will this be?" Let us take the sections as Jesus gives them, and remember that if we want the full account of what he said to the disciples, we must read Matthew 24 and 25 and Luke 21, which are the accounts parallel to Mark's account of what Jesus said here to the disciples. It takes all those passages to give us the full picture. Each of the Gospel writers selects certain things he wants to emphasize. Matthew makes a great deal over what happens to Israel. Luke is the only one who tells us of the fall of Jerusalem and the subsequent captivity of the Jews and domination of the city by the gentiles. But Mark is the one who emphasizes the danger to faith which is going to arise in the age which follows the crucifixion and resurrection of our Lord. Jesus sums it all up in one brief sentence right at the beginning: "And Jesus began to say to them, 'Take heed that no one leads you astray' " (Mk. 13:5).

This is the emphasis he makes—the keynote. You notice that his message begins and ends with that emphasis. He says here, "Take heed," a word which means, "Keep awake." And the final word of the passage is, "Watch," which means, "Don't fall asleep." So at the beginning he says, "Keep awake," and at the end he says, "Don't fall asleep." This is the emphasis he wants to leave during the whole course of the age.

In the first section which follows, from verse 6 through verse

13, Jesus gives us certain "non-signs"; certain things which have deceived people throughout the ages about the coming of the Lord, things which they have taken to be signs but which are not signs at all. I am sure you have read books or have heard sermons based upon these so-called "signs of the times." But they really are not signs, as Jesus makes clear.

The first of these so-called "signs," which many look to as marking the coming of the end, is the coming of various religious pretenders, false Christs. In verse 6 Jesus says, "Many will come in my name, saying, 'I am he!' and they will lead many astray." Dr. Charles Feinberg, a noted Jewish Christian scholar, says that in the course of Israel's history since the time of our Lord, sixty-four different individuals appeared claiming to be the Messiah. So it is true, as Jesus said, many shall come saying, "I am the Messiah; I am he."

But I do not think we need to limit this to those who come to the Jews. It also refers to all in these twenty centuries who claim to speak in the name of Jesus but who teach something that Jesus did not teach. This happens very frequently. In the San Francisco Bay area where I live, I frequently notice automobile bumper stickers which say, "Bless Man." This is a locally based movement which announces that it is following the teachings of Jesus and comes in the name of Jesus. But the "Jesus" it presents is not the biblical Jesus. The teachings of Jesus which they present are a selection culled from all the biblical sayings of Jesus but including only those doctrines which this movement accepts. Many things that Jesus said are not included at all. They have selected certain moral precepts and ethical teachings of Jesus, and they call them "the teachings of Jesus," but this is a distortion of the biblical picture of Jesus. In every age there have been many who have been misled by this kind of presentation.

Most of the so-called "Christian" cults do this. They come in the name of Jesus, but what they teach is not what Jesus taught. They are coming and saying, in effect, "I am he." But

what they teach is a far cry from the biblical presentation of
the Lord Jesus. This, Jesus said, is a deceptive device designed
to lead many astray. And many will be led astray. His word of
warning here is, "Take note of this. Take heed. Be careful that
the Jesus you follow is the biblical Jesus, the apostolic Christ,
the One of whom the apostles give witness, or else you will be
led astray." This has been true through twenty centuries of
history.

## The End Is Not Yet

The second category of "signs" is given in the next two
verses. The Lord says,

> "And when you hear of wars and rumors of wars, do not be
> alarmed; this must take place, but the end is not yet. For nation
> will rise against nation, and kingdom against kingdom; there
> will be earthquakes in various places, there will be famines; this
> is but the beginning of the sufferings" (Mk. 13:7–8).

Those words make very clear that wars, famines, earth-
quakes, and all kinds of natural disasters will occur throughout
the whole sweep of the age. But they are not signs of the times.
They are not signs that the Lord is about to come. Yet if you
read the record of history, you will find that over and over
again people have misunderstood this and have taken them to
be signs. I read books, when I was a young Christian, which
showed that World War I was the fulfillment of this word,
"nation shall rise against nation, and kingdom against kingdom." The books said, "No other war in history has fulfilled
that to this extent. Therefore, this is the sign of the end." Then
World War II came along and they had to explain that. So
they said, "World War I fulfilled the part about 'nation shall
rise against nation' and World War II fulfilled 'kingdom
against kingdom.'" Unfortunately, this is the way expositors
have dealt with this text. But Jesus says that none of those are

signs. There have been wars and rumors of wars right from the very beginning. There are going to be famines and earth-quakes in various places throughout history.

I remember as a lad reading a book about the San Francisco earthquake. I read it with great fascination because it recounted the story of the 1906 earthquake in great detail. But its thesis was, "This is the sign of the end!" I expected the Lord to come the very next day after I finished reading the book! That must have been over forty years ago, and yet he has not returned. But I did not understand then, as I do now, that Jesus said these were not signs; these were but the beginning of the sufferings. We cannot say that the increase of natural disasters is a mark of the end times.

There is another occurrence that is often listed as indicating the end time—the persecution of Christians. Jesus said,

> "But take heed to yourselves; for they will deliver you up to councils; and you will be beaten in synagogues; and you will stand before governors and kings for my sake, to bear testimony before them. And the gospel must first be preached to all na-tions. And when they bring you to trial and deliver you up, do not be anxious beforehand what you are to say; but say whatever is given to you in that hour, for it is not you who speak, but the Holy Spirit" (Mk. 13:9–11).

This is a persecuting age from the very beginning. Right from the very first century these words were fulfilled. The book of Acts tells us how the apostle Paul, other apostles, and the early Christians were often beaten in the synagogues and dragged before governors and kings to give testimony before them.

Mark, you notice, links these events in some way with the preaching of the gospel, so someone says, "Surely this world-wide preaching of the gospel is a sign of the end, and ours is the first generation in which this has occurred." But notice that right in the midst of this statement about being brought before governors and kings, Mark says the gospel is to be preached, indicating that there is some tie between these. This would suggest that when the gospel has penetrated a nation to the extent that it comes to the attention of the governing authorities—who then demand an accounting from those who preach the gospel—then the gospel has been given as a testimony to that nation. When Paul stood before Nero, emperor of Rome, about A.D. 67, that was an indication that the gospel had penetrated much of the Roman empire and had served as a witness to the nations of the world of that day.

Whenever Christians have been brought before governors and kings, God the Holy Spirit has given them special words to speak of witness and testimony, as Jesus promises in this account. Remember how Paul spoke with such wisdom when he stood before King Agrippa and Felix and Festus, the Roman governors. And Martin Luther, standing before the emperor of the Holy Roman Empire, in the city of Worms, was given words to speak which have come ringing down the centuries since: "Here I stand. God help me; I can do no other." Other martyrs and witnesses have been given special wisdom to speak in their hour, as a testimony to the nations. But this is not a sign of the end because it has been going on through the whole course of the age, and it will characterize the age until its end.

Along with this, Jesus points out that this persecution is of such an intense nature that it constitutes a real threat to faith. The anguish of such persecution is that it involves the betrayal of family members one by another. He says,

"And brother will deliver up brother to death, and the father his child, and children will rise against parents and have them put to death; and you will be hated by all for my name's sake. But he who endures to the end will be saved" (Mk. 13:12–13).

Now, "the end" he is talking about there is not the end of the tribulation; it is the end of an individual's life. All Christians are called on to be faithful unto death. Did you realize that? In the book of Revelation, Jesus calls upon the churches to whom he is writing to "be faithful unto death, and I will give you the crown of life." That is not a word for martyrs only, but for all Christians. "Be faithful till your dying day." Why? "Because he who endures to the end will be saved"—not because he has earned his salvation by enduring to the end but because he has proved that he has real life by enduring to the end. Only genuine Christians will survive the test of the age.

In his first letter, John says of certain individuals, "They went out from us, but they were not of us; for if they had been of us, they would have continued with us; but they went out, that it might be plain that they all are not of us" (1 John 2: 19). Every age witnesses those seeming Christians who begin well, seem to be bright and happy and committed, but who begin to fade away under the pressures and tensions of the times. As those tensions and pressures increase, sometimes to the severing of the dearest family ties, there are many who turn back and thus reveal that they never really had life from Christ. This is why we have those passages such as that in Hebrews 6 which warn us that we are to be sure that the life we have is real, genuine, founded in Jesus Christ. For he who endures to the end will be saved.

In the second section we come to the Lord's answer to the question of the disciples regarding signs. They asked, "What will be the sign when these things are all to be accomplished?" Every age longs to know this. Our Lord puts it in one brief phrase:

> "When you see the desolating sacrilege set up where it ought not to be [and I think it was Jesus who added] (let the reader understand)" . . . [but it may have been Mark] (Mk. 13:14).

This parenthetic statement is a reference to the fact that we need to think about this. Matthew tells us that Jesus is referring to the book of Daniel. That is, "Let the reader understand the book of Daniel." For Daniel talks about a desolating sacrilege, an "abomination of desolation," which is to be set up in the temple and will defile and profane the temple. In 2 Thessalonians the apostle Paul evidently is referring to that very sacrilege when he speaks of the "man of sin" who is to appear, who will take his seat in the temple of God, proclaiming that he himself is God. This is the world-wide religion of the last days—the claim that man is God, that we do not need any other God, that man himself is sufficient to his own ends. This religion will be personified in a person who sits in the temple of God.

This is why Bible students have always watched with great interest the possibility of the reconstruction of the temple in Jerusalem. In A.D. 70, the Roman armies of Titus fulfilled the prophecies of Jesus by destroying the temple completely. There has never been a temple in Jerusalem since that day. But Jesus speaks of a desolating sacrilege which will be set up in the temple, which means there must again be a temple in Jerusalem. And as we approach the time when a temple can be constructed, we are seeing the possibility of the fulfillment of that event in our day and age. Now, we are not the first. There have been other times when a temple could have been constructed in Jerusalem—during the Crusades, perhaps. But again in our age there is a very real possibility of its coming to pass. So this may be the beginning of a true sign of the times.

## Sudden Peril

Jesus says that when this appears, there will be three immediate, tremendous—but terrible—results. First, there will be an immediate and sudden peril to those believers who are in Jerusalem and the surrounding area. You tourists to the Holy Land, take note!

". . . then let those who are in Judea flee to the mountains; let him who is on the housetop not go down, nor enter his house, to take anything away; and let him who is in the field not turn back to take his mantle. And alas for those who are with child and for those who give suck in those days! Pray that it may not happen in winter" (Mk. 13:14–18).

It will be a time of such imminent danger that people will have no time even to go home and pack, but they must leave the city promptly or be trapped. The second result is the outbreak of a world-wide time of tribulation:

"For in those days there will be such tribulation as has not been from the beginning of the creation which God created until now, and never will be. And if the Lord had not shortened the days, no human being would be saved; but for the sake of the elect, whom he chose, he shortened the days" (Mk. 13:19–20).

This will be a terrible time of unprecedented trouble. If you want the vivid details of this, read the passages in Revelation which deal with the pouring out of the vials of the wrath of God and the opening of the seven seals and the sounding of the seven trumpets. It will be a time of economic crunch, when all commerce is controlled by a central authority and everyone will be issued a number by which to do business. Perhaps you have read accounts of the computer system already set up in Belgium and designed to issue a number to everyone in the world in order to facilitate the transaction of various forms of business. I do not say that this is necessarily the fulfillment of this prophecy because every age seems to bring us close to it and then to back away. Perhaps we will back away again, who knows? But it could be fulfilled in this day, and this is why we need to take note of these developments. The third result will be:

"And then if any one says to you, 'Look here is the Christ!' or 'Look, there he is!' do not believe it. False Christs and false prophets will arise and show signs and wonders, to lead astray, if possible, the elect. But take heed; I have told you all things beforehand" (Mk. 13:21–23).

This will be a time of world-wide religious deceit. I think we must see these false Christs and false prophets who are mentioned here as the agents of the single supreme anti-Christ who rules and reigns in that day. These are people all over the world who are delegated to bring men and women into submission and subjection to the world-wide religion whose creed is "Man is God." What a threat to faith that is! We can see the beginnings of it in our own time in the constant increase in secularism, though as I have said, there have been such trends in the past. But this may be the one which leads to this final world-wide deceit by the agents of anti-Christ. Then, Jesus says, comes the climax:

> "But in those days, after the tribulation [after and not before], the sun will be darkened, and the moon will not give its light, and the stars will be falling from heaven, and the powers in the heavens will be shaken. And they will see the Son of man coming in clouds with great power and glory. And then he will send out the angels, and gather his elect from the four winds, from the ends of the earth to the ends of heaven" (Mk. 13:24–27).

There is the climax of history—the appearing of Jesus Christ as Lord with great power and great glory. (This is not at all touching the question of the "rapture," the departure of the church. That is dealt with in other passages.) Here we have the appearance again of Jesus Christ in great power and glory, preceded, as all the prophets have predicted, by terrible signs in the heavens. Evidently, some tremendous cataclysm upsets the whole solar system of which we are a part, or perhaps even the entire galaxy. It has been interesting to me that astronomers today are commenting upon newly-discovered forces at work in the heavens and strange, inexplicable heavenly bodies which no one seems to know much about—mysterious "black holes" in space—and "quasars" which emit tremendous amounts of energy, yet seem to be so far removed from the earth that nobody can be quite sure what they are. From other passages we know that this disruption of heavenly bodies will have an effect upon the earth, as volcanoes erupt and tidal waves arise. Then the Son of man appears, and all his mighty angels are with him. He sends those angels out to gather Israel back into the land. This gathering of the elect, I am sure, is the fulfillment of the predictions of the prophets that there will come a time when Israel will be gathered from the four corners of the earth—not by natural but by supernatural means—to establish the kingdom of God there in the land.

## Sacrilege to Glory

Then our Lord gives us a section which draws an analogy from nature:

> "From the fig tree learn its lesson: as soon as its branch becomes tender and puts forth its leaves, you know that summer is near. So also, when you see these things taking place, you know that he is near, at the very gates. Truly, I say to you, this generation will not pass away before all things take place. Heaven and earth will pass away, but my words will not pass away" (Mk. 13:28–31).

This is easy to follow. When you see the trees in the spring putting forth leaves, you know two things for sure. One, summer is very near. It will not be long until the days are warm and the cold weather is over. Second, it is certain. Nothing is going to stop it. When the leaves appear on the trees, summer is certain to come. Jesus says we 'n draw the same conclusions from seeing the events he outlines here coming to pass, for he says, "So also, when you see these things taking place, know that he is near." What does he mean, "these things"? I do not think he means the signs in the heavens, for they are not the beginning of the events. Rather, he is talking about the sign on earth, i.e., the appearance of the desolating sacrilege in the temple in Jerusalem. When you see things beginning to move in this direction, things which begin to make possible this event, then you know that the Lord is drawing near—so near, in fact, that Jesus says, "Truly, I say to you, this generation will not pass away before all these things take place." That is, once it starts, it will all be over before a generation has run its course. A generation is about twenty-seven years.

And, it is also certain. How certain? "Heaven and earth will pass away, but my words will not pass away." Those words are given to us to undergird our faith in a time of testing, a time when it seems that perhaps the biblical record is just a dream and cannot be trusted. In such a time, remember these words of Jesus: "Heaven and earth will pass away"—as solid and real as they appear—but these words will not pass away. This is absolutely certain to happen. History is going to end this way. Remember this, regardless of what secular voices are saying around you.

In the last section Jesus answers the question of when this shall happen: "But of that day or that hour no one knows, not even the angels in heaven, nor the Son, but only the Father" (Mk. 13:32). This means that anybody who claims to have a revelation as to when this event is going to take place has been deluded. Even the angels do not know. The fallen angels do not know, and even the true, the holy angels do not know.

## No Way to Tell

Then comes perhaps the most startling thing Jesus ever said: "Nor does the Son; I don't know." This marks the humanity of our Lord. He laid aside the prerogative of deity when he came to earth and never exercised it while he was here. He was a man like us, limited to the knowledge that God made known to him. God had not told him this, so he did not know. He said, "I don't know the answer; only the Father knows." Remember that even after his resurrection he said to his disciples, "The times and the seasons are not for you to know. [Quit trying to find out!] But the Father has put them in his own power." So the question of when is not important because it cannot be determined. There is no way that you can tell the day or the hour. And as we read on, we will see that our Lord did not even know how long it was going to be before he came back. All these disciples thought it would take place within their lifetime, and Jesus seems to speak as though that were the case: "When you see the desolating sacrilege," etc. But it did not happen then. I do not think Jesus himself could have told us how long he would be gone. It has been almost two thousand years, and in all that time no one has known when he would come. He says,

> "Take heed, watch; [That is the important thing.] for you do not know when the time will come. It is like a man going on a journey, when he leaves home and puts his servants in charge, each with his work, and commands the doorkeeper to be on the watch. Watch therefore—for you do not know when the master of the house will come, in the evening, or at midnight, or at cockcrow, or in the morning—lest he come suddenly and find you asleep. And what I say to you I say to all: Watch" (Mk. 13:33–37).

Here he gathers up all the intervening time between his first and second comings and divides it into four watches—one long night of the world's sin—and he says, "You don't know. (And I think he implies, "I don't know.") whether the coming is to be early in that time, or in the middle of it, or three-quarters of the way through, or clear at the end. No one knows. I don't know; you don't know. But it is like a man going on a journey (Here he likens it to his own going away.) who gives his servants work to do, and he expects them to do it. And he sets a doorkeeper to watch."

Now, what is he to watch for? Is he to watch for the master's return? That is the way this is usually interpreted. But that is not it, for he is to start watching as soon as the master leaves.

They know he will not be back right away. What then is he to
watch for? He is to watch lest somebody deceive them and gain
entrance into the house and wreck and ruin and rob all they
have. So Jesus' word is, "Be alert; don't go to sleep; watch!
There are temptations and pressures which will assault you, to
make you think that it is all a lie, to make you give up and stop
living like a Christian—stop walking in faith, stop believing
the truth of God. Watch out for that. And, in the meantime,
do your work. Don't let anything turn you aside. Don't let anything derail you from being what God wants you to be in this
day and age." This is the way you watch. We are not to be
looking up into the sky all the time, waiting for his coming.
That will happen when he is ready. We are to watch that we
are not deceived.

I have been disturbed at how many Christians of late seem
to have fallen away. When I look back across thirty years of
ministry, I see men whom I would have sworn were solid, tremendously committed, faithful, Bible-teaching Christians, but
they are now denying their faith and have turned aside. And
on every side, seemingly, this increases—people falling off into
immorality and iniquity, turning away from their faith, saying,
in effect, they no longer believe the Lord or the Bible. It is this
our Lord is warning against. Therefore, he says we are to keep
awake. Do not believe all the secular voices that tell us the
world will go on forever as it is now. Don't believe the other
voices which tell us there is no God so we can live as we please,
or that if God exists, he will never judge us. Don't believe the
voices which whisper to us constantly and try to turn us away
from our faith. With one sharp, arresting, ringing word of command, Jesus ends his message: "Watch!"

# 11

# Love's Extravagance

In the fourteenth chapter Mark does what he has done frequently throughout this Gospel—he brings together certain events and themes which occurred at various times during this week and deliberately places them side by side so that we might see his emphases through contrasts. Like an artist, he draws together two lines of truth, taking that line of thought which centers around hate and that which centers around love and braids them together. Mark's account of the hatred of the priests toward Jesus is followed by the story of the love toward him of Mary of Bethany. Then you come to the story of Judas' mounting hatred and enmity against Jesus, followed by the story of Jesus' love for his disciples as exhibited at their last Passover together. These two themes are mingled together in the disclosure by Jesus of the betrayal of Judas at the table of the Lord. We begin with the words which set forth the hatred of the priests:

It was now two days before the Passover and the feast of Unleavened Bread. And the chief priests and the scribes were seek-

ing how to arrest him by stealth, and kill him; for they said,
"Not during the feast, lest there be a tumult of the people"
(Mk. 14:1–2).

These priests are aware, as Mark makes known here, that
time is growing short, that if they are going to act, they must
act now. The days of the Passover and the Feast of the Unleavened Bread are at hand. Josephus tells us that at these
Passover feasts there were sometimes as many as three million
people in Jerusalem and the surrounding villages—pilgrims
from all parts of the earth. The Passover could be celebrated
only in Jerusalem, so the city was thronged with strangers from
various parts of the world. The chief priests and scribes know
that if they take Jesus at the height of the feast, they are apt to
incite a riot, so they want to act beforehand. As there are only
two days left, there is a deep sense of urgency about their
malevolent threat. This is always characteristic of hatred. Hatred can never wait, but must act as soon as an opportunity
presents itself.

Mark makes clear, too, that these priests were motivated by
a sense of threat to their own position. Why did they want to
kill Jesus? Because his system of teaching and his whole style
of living was a threat to them. They were trying to pose as
God's men, religious men, men whose interests and concerns
were to relieve the distress and suffering of others. But when
Jesus taught, he exposed them. He cut through their hypocrisy
and showed what liars they were, so they were out to get him.

Mark shows us also that there is a definite air of secrecy on
their part. They have to move by stealth; this also is always
characteristic of hatred. Hatred moves behind the scenes; it
does not come out into the open if it can help it.

## Loving Sacrifice

In sharp contrast, Mark next gives us the account of what
took place in Bethany. It actually took place a few days before

this, for John tells us it was six days before the Passover. Mark
is simply recounting it, not in chronological order but as something he sets in contrast with the hatred of the priests. It is the
story of the love of Mary of Bethany:

> And while he was at Bethany in the house of Simon the leper,
> as he sat at table, a woman came with an alabaster jar of oint-
> ment of pure nard, very costly, and she broke the jar and poured
> it over his head. But there were some who said to themselves
> indignantly, "Why was the ointment thus wasted? For this oint-
> ment might have been sold for more than three hundred denarii,
> and given to the poor." And they reproached her. But Jesus
> said, "Let her alone; why do you trouble her? She has done a
> beautiful thing to me. For you always have the poor with you,
> and whenever you will, you can do good to them; but you will
> not always have me. She has done what she could; she has
> anointed my body beforehand for burying. And truly, I say to
> you, wherever the gospel is preached in the whole world, what
> she has done will be told in memory of her" (Mk. 14:3–9).

Here we have a wonderful account of the love of this
woman. Mark does not give her name, but John tells us it was
Mary, the sister of Martha and Lazarus, who seized this occasion to anoint the head of Jesus. There are three movements in
this brief account. The first is the act of loving sacrifice. You
can picture it in your imagination: Mary coming into the room
with a jar of expensive ointment as Jesus is reclining on the
couch. John tells us that she anointed both his head and his
feet, which were both easily accessible to her as he lay, oriental
fashion, on the couch beside the table. She breaks the jar and
pours the whole contents upon his head and feet, anointing him.
It is a beautiful act, one which captures the attention of all
those present.

Second, it awakened a response. Mark tells us the first response was one of indignation that she should waste this ointment. John says it was Judas who raised this objection, which

was characteristic of Judas; he would be likely to be concerned only about the waste of money. John says he was a thief. He had been appointed treasurer for the disciples—not because he was a thief but because he was good at money. Nevertheless, he became a thief as a result. There are always people who try to place a monetary value on things. They seem to know the price of everything but the value of nothing. In this account Jesus is warning us of the foolishness of that attitude, for if you look at the world only in terms of dollars and cents, you are going to miss three-quarters of life. This is one thing he wants to teach us here.

Third, our Lord takes this beautiful incident and shows us the true value of it. He says five things about it which mark it as an extremely valuable act. First he says, "She has done a beautiful thing to me." The beauty of it lay in its very extravagance. This woman did not spare any of the ointment, but she broke the flask and poured the whole quantity out upon him. Now, it was costly ointment. Judas, with his practical, computer mind reckoned it up as worth three hundred denarii. A denarius was the day's wage for a laborer. In these inflated times, three hundred days' wages would be a tremendous sum —probably at least $10,000. But in those days, a denarius was worth about 20 cents, so that would make this ointment worth approximately $60.00—almost a year's wages. In the eyes of Judas, this woman wasted an enormous amount of money when she poured out the ointment upon Jesus. It was such a lavish act, and therein lay the beauty of it. Jesus said, "That's beautiful! She hasn't held anything back, but has simply poured it all out. It's a beautiful thing she has done to me."

Second, he said that it was a timely thing she had done. "It was something that could only be done now. Anytime you want to do good to the poor you can because they are always around." And it is right to help the poor. But there are opportunities which come in life which must be seized at the moment; they never happen again. Mary had sensed this and had seized the moment to do this which could only have been done then, for such a time would never occur again. It was out of the sensitivity of her heart that she realized that the timing was right, and Jesus recognized this.

## The Only Possibility

Then, she did that which was feasible. That is, she did what she could. It was all that was open to her. She could not fix him a meal; there was no time for that. She could not make a garment for him; there was no time for that. There was nothing else she could do to show her love but this, and so this is what she did. She did what she could. I like that. I am sure our Lord has called our attention to it because it is so practical for us. Someone has said, "I'm only a man, but I *am* a man. I can't do everything, but I *can* do something. And what I can do I *ought* to do. And what I ought to do, I'm available to do."

This is really the attitude the Lord asks of all of us. You cannot do everything. You cannot feed the starving world, but you can feed one person. You cannot comfort all the lonely hearts on earth, but you can comfort one or two. And Mary did what she could. Everywhere in Scripture, this is all God asks us—that we bring him what is at hand. Perhaps you think you live a dull life and you never have an opportunity for real service. But you do! This is what this story tells us. There is something that you can do today. And in doing it with the expectation that God will take it and enlarge it, you will find that tremendous results can follow. We are to bring our loaves and fishes—a simple little meal—and Jesus will feed the multitude. We must fill the jars with water, but he will turn it into wine. When we do what we can, with the expectation that God will use it, what a beautiful expression it is!

The fourth element of this act was that it was insightful. Our Lord says, "She has anointed my body beforehand for burying." It is interesting to go through the Gospel accounts and note the many times Jesus told his disciples that he was

going to die. Over and over again he informed them that he
was heading for death. Not one of them believed him—except
Mary of Bethany. She believed him and understood that he was
here for that very purpose. This was what motivated her. She
understood that he was heading for burial. Just as love would
long to do some service for him, since she could not be sure she
would ever have the opportunity later to find his body and
anoint it for burial in the Jewish custom, she did it now. I
think it is clear from this account that Jesus knew she did this
deliberately for that very purpose. What a comfort this must
have been to our Lord! Of all these friends who were around
him at this time, only this one had the sensitivity of heart to
understand what was happening. There is nothing more comforting to us than to be understood in what we are trying to do.
How she must have ministered to him by this understanding
act!

Finally, what she did was memorable. Jesus said, "The story
of this beautiful act will be told in memory of her wherever
the gospel is preached in the whole world." Here we are today, 2,000 years later, fulfilling this very word, telling again
of the act of Mary of Bethany when she anointed our Lord's
head and feet. Those elements constitute what Jesus called,
"The beautiful thing she has done to me."

## One of the Twelve

Immediately in contrast to that is the hatred of Judas:

Then Judas Iscariot, who was one of the twelve, went to the
chief priests in order to betray him to them. And when they
heard it they were glad, and promised to give him money. And
he sought an opportunity to betray him (Mk. 14:10–11).

This is probably one of the saddest portions of the record
of Judas—this shabby moment when he went to the high
priests deliberately intending to find an occasion to betray the
Lord. There are some scholars today who try to excuse Judas.

They say that he was merely misled. Judas expected Christ to usher in the Kingdom, and he had this program in view for him. And since Jesus did not act in line with that, Judas was simply trying to force his hand. And though he was mistaken, nevertheless, he was not evil-intentioned. But this account refutes that. He went deliberately to the high priests—took the initiative—with the intention of betraying his Lord. Mark highlights it with these words: "he was one of the twelve." He was of the inner circle, the ones upon whom Jesus leaned and depended, and yet he went to betray his Lord.

He did it, Mark says, because of greed, covetousness. Here again is that sense of urgency which hatred always exhibits. It has got to be done quickly. And because it is evil, it has to be done in secret as well. He went in secret, motivated by a deep sense of greed. If we put all the Gospel accounts together, we can see that he had a little scheme of his own. He had been stealing from the treasury in order to purchase for himself a piece of land that would be his when he came into the Kingdom. He needed a little more money, just thirty pieces of silver, and it was that for which he bargained with the priests in order to complete his purchase. It was nothing but common, ordinary greed that drove Judas to this deliberate, cold act of betrayal.

Once again, now, Mark brings in the thread of the theme of love. In the closing account of this section he shows us the love of Jesus as he brings about this last Passover feast. Again there are three movements: first, the preparation for the Passover, beginning in verse 12:

> And on the first day of Unleavened Bread, when they sacrificed the passover lamb, his disciples said to him, "Where will you have us go and prepare for you to eat the passover?" And he sent two of his disciples, and said to them, "Go into the city, and a man carrying a jar of water will meet you; follow him, and wherever he enters, say to the householder, 'The Teacher says, Where is my guest room, where I am to eat the passover

with my disciples?' And he will show you a large upper room
furnished and ready; there prepare for us." And the disciples set
out and went to the city, and found it as he had told them: and
they prepared the passover (Mk. 14:12–16).


Again, just as in the case of the arrangements regarding the
donkey he rode into Jerusalem, I do not think we need to read
anything miraculous into this signal Jesus gave his disciples as
to how to find the upper room. These were both prearranged—
preparations he had worked out in advance. But there is sig-
nificance in them because he deliberately planned that this
should be the signal. He said, "When you go into the city, you
will find a man carrying a jar of water." Now, that would
stand out like a man today carrying a purse on his arm, for
this was woman's work. Only women carried jars of water on
their heads. A man might consent to carry a skin of water, but
not a jar. Jars belonged to women. They had their divisions of
labor in those days just as we have today. He told them, "You
won't have any difficulty, because you will find a man carrying
a jar of water; follow him." And they found it to be just as he
said.

Why did he use this symbol? I cannot read this without
being convinced that our Lord arranged it this way because he
wanted to say something by it. God's symbols always have
meaning if we know how to understand and read them. We do
not need even to guess at what he is saying here—the Scriptures tell us what this symbol meant. There is another feast of
the Jews which centers around the carrying of a jar of water by
a man. It is the Feast of Tabernacles, which is referred to in
John's Gospel. The celebration of that feast involved men—the
priests—carrying water daily to be poured out on the altar. In
the seventh chapter of John Jesus stood up at that feast and
said to the whole crowd, "If anyone thirst, let him come to me
and drink. He who believes in me, as the Scripture has said,
'Out of his heart shall flow rivers of living water.' " I think this

is what he is saying here to his disciples. "Where we are going you don't understand. Although some of the symbolism of this feast of the Passover lamb is known to you, there are other elements of it that you do not know. But follow me, and out of your hearts shall flow rivers of living water."

Then we come to the second movement, the upper room itself:

> And when it was evening he came with the twelve. And as they were at table eating, Jesus said, "Truly, I say to you, one of you will betray me, one who is eating with me." They began to be sorrowful, and to say to him one after another, "Is it I?" He said to them, "It is one of the twelve, one who is dipping bread in the same dish with me. For the Son of man goes as it is written of him, but woe to that man by whom the Son of man is betrayed! It would have been better for that man if he had not been born" (Mk. 14:17–21).

I think our imagination of this occasion, the initiation of the Lord's last supper, is often misled by Leonardo da Vinci's painting. We have seen that painting so often that we imagine these men gathered around the table as de Vinci pictured it. In fact, as someone has said, it looks as though Jesus had just said to them, "All you fellows who want to get into the picture come over on this side of the table!" But that is not the way it was. They were not seated around the table, and they certainly were not seated on just three sides of the table. They were lying on couches around a low table in the Roman custom, which the Jews of this time also observed. In that arrangement, the head of John the disciple lay close to the breast of Jesus. But on the other side of Jesus, equally close to him, was Judas, so that the head of Jesus lay near the breast of Judas. This must have been the arrangement in order to allow for the interchange that went on at the table. When Jesus said, "It is the one who is dipping bread in the same dish with me who is going to betray me," there were only two of the disciples who could have reached the same dish that Jesus used—John and Judas. What he was saying to the other disciples was that it was one of those two.

And yet, forever to the credit of these disciples, when Jesus said, "It is one of you twelve who is going to betray me," not one of them pointed his finger at any other in accusation. Instead, they looked at Jesus and said, "Lord, is it I?" Every one of us recognizes the feeling that there is something evil in us, something we do not trust, something we are not sure will not break out sometime and carry us into acts that appall us—deeds we are aghast at the thought of doing. Something of that self-distrust gripped these men at that moment, and they said, "Is it I?" But Jesus reassured them, said, "No, it is the one who is dipping his hand in the dish with me."

Other accounts tell us that shortly after this he said to Judas privately, "What you are about to do, go and do quickly." And Judas left the company. But before he left, Jesus said to these disciples, "The Son of man goes as it is written of him," i.e., it had been predicted that he would be betrayed by one of his own, and this was being fulfilled. But, and this is important to notice, Jesus also said, "Woe to that man by whom the Son of man is betrayed!" Woe to him!—not because he is doing something he cannot help doing, because he could have helped it. Judas was not driven to betray the Lord; he chose to do so. This is why Jesus adds what are probably the most solemn words that ever fell from his lips: "It would have been better for that man if he had never been born." I do not think that any more fearful words ever came from the lips of Jesus. Wouldn't you hate to have him say that about you?

## The Precious Ointment

But now, the last scene:

And as they were eating, he took bread, and blessed, and broke it, and gave it to them, and said, "Take; this is my body." And he took a cup, and when he had given thanks he gave it to them, and they all drank of it. And he said to them, "This is my blood of the new covenant, which is poured out for many. Truly, I say to you, I shall not drink again of the fruit of the vine until that day when I drink it new in the kingdom of God" (Mk. 14: 22–25).

This obviously is symbolism. Our Lord is teaching again by means of symbols, but the symbols are very significant. He took the bread and said, "This is my body," and he broke the bread, symbolizing how his body would be broken. And he took the cup, and said, "This is the blood of the new covenant," i.e., the new agreement that God makes with men—by faith and not by works; by believing and not by performance. That is the New Covenant. Then he reminded them that this was the end, that he would never drink of the cup again until he drank it new in the fulfillment of the kingdom of God.

Now we can understand why Mark has put this account alongside the story of Mary of Bethany. For here our Lord is showing these disciples that he was doing to them what Mary had done to him. She brought a beautiful alabaster flask, and she broke it. He said, "My body is that flask, and I am going to be broken for you." She poured out of the flask all the ointment that was in it so that the fragrance of it filled the room, as it has filled the earth in the centuries since. And Jesus said, "I will pour out of the flask of my body [what Peter calls] 'the precious blood', all of it, for you, that the fragrance of it may fill your life, and fill the whole earth."

One of the most powerfully moving films I have ever seen is a movie called "The Hiding Place." In the midst of it is a scene set in the Ravensbruck concentration camp in Germany. Corrie Ten Boom and her sister Betsie are there along with ten thousand other women in the horribly degrading, hideous conditions of this camp. They are gathered with some of the women in the barracks in the midst of the beds, cold and hungry and lice-ridden, and Betsie is leading a Bible class. One of the other women calls out derisively from her bunk and mocks their worship of God. They fall into a conversation, and this woman says what so frequently is flung at Christians: "If your God is such a good God, why does he allow this kind of suffering?" Dramatically, she tears off the bandages and old rags that bind her hands, displaying her broken, mangled fingers and says, "I'm the first violinist of the Symphony Orchestra. Did your God will this?" For a moment no one answers. Then Corrie Ten Boom steps to the side of her sister and says, in simple words, "We can't answer that question. All we know is that our God came to this earth, and became one of us, and he suffered with us and was crucified and died. And that he did it for love."

That is what this story is saying to us. This is love's extravagance. When we partake of the table of the Lord together, Jesus is saying, "It is I who break the flask of my own body to pour out upon you all the precious ointment so that you may understand that it is no longer law which governs your life; it is love."

# 12

# Smite the Shepherd

I am sure that the twenty-third Psalm, the Shepherd's Psalm, is the best-loved psalm of all. I know thousands of people who have been helped and strengthened by those opening words, "The Lord is my shepherd, I shall not want." The thought of the Lord as shepherd of his people—watching over his flock, guarding them, protecting them, leading them into green pastures, and making them to lie down beside the still water—has comforted many. Fulfilling this psalm must have been much in our Lord's thoughts as he gathered with his disciples in the upper room. Mark indicates this by the words with which he describes the close of the supper and the progress of the Lord and his disciples on their way to Gethsemane:

And when they had sung a hymn, they went out to the Mount of Olives. And Jesus said to them, "You will all fall away; for it is written, 'I will strike the shepherd, and the sheep will be scattered.' But after I am raised up, I will go before you to Galilee." Peter said to him, "Even though they all fall away, I will not." And Jesus said to him, "Truly, I say to you, this very night, before the cock crows twice, you will deny me three times." But he said vehemently, "If I must die with you, I will not deny you." And they all said the same (Mk. 14:26–31).

There are two things to note in this brief paragraph. First, the passage reveals very clearly how Jesus knew what was going to happen to him. It has been suggested before this, through various incidents, that the Lord seemed to understand fully what the divine program is, anticipated it, even made arrangements for it. I am sure that as he thought and meditated on these events and prayed about them before the Father, the Spirit made known to him details not recorded in Scripture, so that it was clear to him what was going to happen. For example, the very hymn that Jesus and the disciples sang as they left the upper room was a part of the Old Testament. Unquestionably, it was the Scripture we now know as Psalms 113 and 118. This was the traditional hymn called the great Hallel that was sung at the close of the Passover Feast. Hallel is Hebrew for "Praise to God," and these psalms focus on one theme: Hallelujah. It is significant that the closing verse of the great Hallel includes these words, "Bind the festal sacrifice with cords to the horns of the altar" (Ps. 118:27, NAS).

## Prediction of Struggle

As they sang those words, they left the upper room and made their way down across the darkness of the Kidron Valley into the shadows of Gethsemane's garden. And as they went, Jesus quoted from the prophecy of Zechariah. He said to them, "You will all fall away; for it is written, 'I will strike the shepherd, and the sheep will be scattered.' " In my earlier study in the book of Hebrews, entitled, "What More Can God Say?" (Regal Press), I say that in my understanding Jesus did not expect what would happen in the Garden of Gethsemane. But in studying through this passage anew I must repudiate that statement. Before, I had not seen clearly how this passage in

Zechariah was intended to be a prediction of Jesus' struggle in the Garden of Gethsemane, as it surely is. Zechariah predicted that Jehovah would say, "Strike the shepherd that the sheep may be scattered." Now when Jesus quoted this, he changed it from the imperative mode, "Strike the shepherd," to the indicative, "I will strike the shepherd." The words come from the lips of God himself. The full verse says, " 'Awake, O sword, against My Shepherd, And against the man who stands next to me,' says the Lord of hosts."

The result of that smiting would be the scattering of the sheep. In Matthew's account of this Jesus adds "this night": "You will all fall away because of me this night; for it is written, 'I will strike the Shepherd . . .' " Therefore, it is very clear that Zechariah was predicting the Garden of Gethsemane. Gethsemane's struggle was the smiting of the Shepherd, and the result would be the scattering of the sheep. You can see how true that is if you look forward a bit to verse 50, where it says of the disciples, "And they all forsook him, and fled." This is the scattering of the sheep. Jesus did understand what was to happen that night in the Garden of Gethsemane.

He is still thinking of himself as the Shepherd when he says these words to the disciples. "But after I am raised up, I will go before you to Galilee." Remember in John 10 where Jesus says, "I am the good shepherd. The good shepherd lays down his life for the sheep." He says of this shepherd, "When he has brought out all his own, he goes before them . . ." He is reassuring his disciples that after the dark event of Calvary there will come the glory of the resurrection. He will go before them as the Shepherd, still guarding his flock, still watching over them, and he will meet them again in Galilee.

Never once did Jesus speak of his cross to these disciples without setting it against the dawning light of the resurrection. And yet they never seemed to grasp it. Not one of them believed Jesus would be raised from the dead. I think that because they did not want to hear about his death, they would

not believe in his resurrection. And so, though he tried to comfort them, his words were of no avail.

The second thing to note about this passage is the confident
bravado of Peter and the disciples. Peter said to Jesus, "Even
though they all fall away, I will not." Notice the contrast between "they" and "I." "They will all deny you." Peter said, "I
know these fellows, Lord, and you can't trust a one of them!
They'll all deny you; you're right about that! But Lord, you're
wrong about me. I will not!" Peter is confident that he will
not do what the rest will do. He is not at all hesitant to point
out that he expects the others to fall, but it is going to be different with him.

But Jesus saw far more clearly than Peter. He saw that
Peter's confidence was resting upon his own human determination, his own will, and Jesus knew the weakness of it. So he
said to him, "Truly, I say to you, this very night, before the
cock crows twice, you will deny me three times." It is interesting to see how Jesus narrows down the time. First he says,
"Truly, I say to you, today . . ." Then he narrows it further,
"this very night," and still further, "before the cock crows
twice." In effect Jesus is saying, "In just a few hours, Peter, all
that firm resolve, all that confident arrogance, all that clenched-
fist determination you have manifested in saying you will not
deny me, is going to melt away, leaving you with no ability to
stand. And it will happen before these few hours have passed."

I am always amazed by the symbols that Jesus employs.
They are so apt, so characteristic. And here is the symbol that
he employs to depict this arrogance and confidence of Peter
and the other disciples: that of a cock, a rooster. It stands forever as a symbol of an attitude like Peter's. We speak of somebody who is cocksure. We call a person "cocky" who is almost
arrogantly confident. Jesus does not say this, but I am sure he
intended for Peter to think about the fate of most cocks: they
lose their heads.

But Peter insisted that Jesus was wrong. He said vehemently,

"If I must die with you, I will not deny you, Lord. I'm prepared to go the whole way! How can you say I will deny you when I am ready, yea, even eager, to give up my life for you?" Peter is so sure that Jesus is wrong. Have you ever felt that way? I have. I have been so sure that something the Word says could not happen. I have been sure that by sheer determination and force of will I could work it out on my own. I have said the same thing Peter did, and so have you. Jesus says the next time you think like this, just remember that cocky little rooster you saw strutting around in the barnyard. That's the same rooster you had for dinner last week!

## The Smiting Begins

Now back to Gethsemane:

> And they went to a place which was called Gethsemane; and he said to his disciples, "Sit here, while I pray." And he took with him Peter and James and John, and began to be greatly distressed and troubled. And he said to them, "My soul is very sorrowful, even to death; remain here, and watch." And going a little farther, he fell on the ground and prayed that, if it were possible, the hour might pass from him. And he said, "Abba, Father, all things are possible to thee; remove this cup from me; yet not what I will, but what thou wilt" (Mk. 14:32–36).

Here begins the terrible smiting Zechariah had predicted. Jehovah called for a sword: "Awake, O sword, against my shepherd. I will strike the shepherd, that the sheep may be scattered." God would do it himself; he would strike his own shepherd, "this man who is my fellow," and the sheep would be scattered. A sword is an instrument designed to sever, to separate. I think that figure explains why here, for the first time in the ministry of our Lord, we have the sense of division between Jesus and the Father. This separation is manifested when Jesus says, "Not my will, but thine be done." Up to this point in our Lord's ministry he knew clearly that he was going to go to the cross. But this is the first sign that he was not

willing and ready to go to the cross. He spoke of it, he understood what it would involve, yet before this point there is no
indication that he was in any way reluctant to go. He had said,
"I delight always to do those things that please the Father."
Even though it involved some degree of hardship or difficulty
for him, he wanted to do it. In the same way, many a young
man can be challenged to do a dangerous or arduous task, and
he delights to do it, though it costs him greatly. So Jesus went
toward the cross with a confident sense that he was in the
Father's will. And though it would be hard and dangerous and
difficult, yea, even deadly, he was willing to do it.

Now all is changed. Suddenly, and it seems to be for the
very first time, Jesus does not want to do what the Father wants
him to do. There is a sense of distance, of deviation. This is
why there came upon his spirit this deep sense of struggle,
distress. The disciples sense this, and he does not try to hide it
from them. He says to them, "My soul is deeply sorrowful
within me, even to the point of death." Now, very few of us
have ever stood at the place where we were so troubled, so
hurting within, so deeply distressed that we feared for our life.
But Jesus was. There was this strange unwillingness to do the
Father's will, even though he knew it was inevitable. He prays,
"Father, if it be possible, let this cup pass from me." There are
some who think that the cup refers to the agony of Gethsemane
itself. But I do not think so, because at the end of this account,
when Jesus is arrested by the soldiers who come with Judas,
Peter wields a sword in his defense. But Jesus says, "Put up
your sword, Peter; shall I not drink the cup which the Father
has given me?" That cup is still ahead, the cup of agony and
terrible separation that he knew awaited him on the cross.

I know there are some Christians who are very troubled by
the idea that there ever was a time when Jesus did not want to
do the Father's will. A man once wrote me a letter saying that
he was very troubled by statements in my study in Hebrews
which said that Jesus did not want to do the Father's will. He

argued that Jesus' statement, "Not my will, but thine," is the
acme of perfect and voluntary submission on his part. It is.
Jesus does want to do the Father's will ultimately, and he does
choose to obey. But the language is evacuated of its content if
you take out all the sense of division and conflict that is in
these words. "Not my will, but thine." Jesus did not want to
obey. Something within him made him dread it, and we can
understand why he wanted to escape it. He asked for a way out,
"if it were at all possible"; yet he added, "not my will, but
thine be done."

## He Learned Obedience

I am greatly helped by this trembling on Jesus' part. And I
think the account in Hebrews 5 also helps us at this point.
Hebrews tells us that this agony was so intense, so severe, that
as Jesus fell upon his face, blood was forced from his veins by
the agony and pressure within so that his sweat fell in great
drops of blood upon the ground. His mouth was opened in in-
voluntary cries of anguish. Hebrews 5:7 says that with strong
crying and tears he pleaded with his Father, the One who was
able to save him from death. And he was heard. I think that is
why Luke's account says an angel appeared to strengthen him.
He was heard for his godly submission. Hebrews 5:8 says, "Although he was a Son, he learned obedience through what he
suffered." That is the meaning of this smiting of the shepherd
in Gethsemane. Hebrews tells us, "For we have not a high
priest who is unable to sympathize with our weaknesses, but
one who in every respect has been tempted as we are, yet without sinning." If he had never felt that divergency of will, that
unwillingness to do what he ought to do because the Father
wanted it, he could never have sympathized with me, because
in my weakness I am frequently unwilling—and so are you.
Jesus did not want to do what the Father wanted him to do.
He had to compel himself to go on. And he did it by casting
himself anew upon his Father's enabling strength. That is

what his prayers in Gethsemane mean. There is much of mystery here. I can go no further into it than that. But yet I see tremendous help here for those of us who struggle with the will of God.

In the congregation in which I am a pastor there is a young couple who separated from one another some years ago, shortly after they were first married. They had a little baby, but after an angry session, the young man took off and left his family. I talked with him at that time, and he told me he hated his wife and she hated him. He did not want ever to go back. We talked a bit about the responsibility he had as a Christian, but he rejected it and went off angry and distressed. But the Spirit of God spoke to him and made him aware that he could not expect God's blessing on his life, or any happiness, if he deliberately refused to obey what God told him to do. So, with every fiber of his being shrieking out against it, he determined that he would obey God and go back to his wife and baby. It was not easy to do, but he did it. And he found that God had done a similar work in his wife's heart, so they came back together with some degree of humility and a willingness to work it out. Gradually, God restored the home and this couple's love for one another. They are still members of this church family and have a beautiful marriage. The husband said he knew he had to go back to his family even though it was contrary to every feeling he had. Jesus understands that. And there will come a time when, no matter what the Word of God says, you do not want to obey. And as Jesus himself has shown us by example, the answer is to cast ourselves afresh upon the mercy and grace of God, knowing that if God does not go with us, it won't work. But we determine to obey on the basis of God's character.

## A Stealthy Sandman

In the next section we see the ease with which Peter's fierce resolve and determination is overcome.

And he came and found them sleeping, and he said to Peter, "Simon, are you asleep? Could you not watch one hour? Watch and pray that you may not enter into temptation; the spirit indeed is willing, but the flesh is weak." And again he went away and prayed, saying the same words. And again he came and found them sleeping, for their eyes were very heavy; and they did not know what to answer him. And he came the third time, and said to them, "Are you still sleeping and taking your rest? It is enough; the hour has come; the Son of man is betrayed into the hands of sinners. Rise, let us be going; see, my betrayer is at hand" (Mk. 14:37–42).

The enemy has very little struggle with Peter. It is not even necessary to threaten to throw him to the lions or burn him at the stake. His resolve collapses by the simple expedient of making him too sleepy to pray. That is all; and that tremendous determination of will, that firm resolve, dissolves, and Peter is as weak as putty when the moment comes. He is weak because he lacks the strengthening of prayer. The devil only had to make him sleepy, that is all. I am sure this was a satanic attack. The sword Jehovah was wielding, and which hurt and distressed the Son of God, was now affecting the disciples, and Satan was allowed to appear as a stealthy sandman, dropping sleep into their eyes. So they fell asleep instead of praying.

Jesus analyzes the situation. He comes and finds them, and there is almost a touch of humor here. After he wakes them up, he says to these disciples, "Peter, couldn't you watch one hour? Couldn't your resolve and fierce determination last at least that long?" Then he tells us why Peter could not do it. "The spirit is willing, Peter, I know your heart. I know you love me. Your spirit is perfectly willing. But Peter, you relied upon your flesh. The flesh is weak."

We have all felt this, have we not? We have been asked to do something and we say, "The spirit is willing, but the flesh is ready for the weekend." The flesh is weak. Jesus says that is the nature of the flesh. That human sense of independence, the confidence we have in ourselves, is always weak in the hour of testing. It cannot stand the test. Jesus said the same thing in Matthew 7 where he used another example, that of building a house. "He that hears my word and does my will is like the man who builds his house upon a rock. But he who hears my word and forgets it is like the man who builds his house upon the sand." In the hour of testing, the house built upon the sand will collapse. It cannot stand the test. The spirit that is confident it can carry through on the basis of sheer grit and determination is going to fail. The arm of flesh will fail you.

This is the analysis Jesus gives of Peter's problem. The key is prayer. If Peter, like Jesus, feeling sleepy and weak, had cast himself upon the Father and told him the problem, the Father would have carried him through, and he would not have denied his Lord. It is our weakness that is our security, not our strength. That is why I am not terribly impressed when young people tell me how much they are going to do for God and how certain they are that they can carry it through. I have learned, out of sad experience in my own life as well as by the testimony of Scripture, that in the hour of testing, this self-confidence will all wash away. But I have confidence in the man or woman who says, "I'm scared. I don't think I can do this, but I'm going to try because God tells me to. I'm looking to him to strengthen me." Prayer is a simple principle, but what a transformation is obtained in our lives when it is practiced. Prayer—what a difference it makes!

During a recent trip to Europe my wife and daughter and I walked around in the great cathedral at Worms, Germany, along the Rhine River. As we walked beneath that imposing gothic structure, we tried to visualize in our mind's eye that scene so long ago when all the powers of Europe were assembled in that place: the Roman emperor in all his robes and dignity; the papal delegates, the bishops and archbishops of all the Catholic realms of Europe. It was the most imposing array of power possible on the face of the earth that day, all gathered in that great cathedral against one lone man, Dr. Martin Luther, who was on trial for his life. The account tells us that the night before someone overheard Martin Luther praying and wrote down the words of his prayer. It was a long, rambling, disconnected prayer of a soul in deep distress and fear, crying out to God for help, casting himself anew, again and again, upon the strength of God, and reminding himself that there is no source of hope or help except God. All his reliance upon the princes of the German state disappeared. Martin Luther cast himself in naked helplessness upon the grace and sustaining strength of God. I am sure that is why, at that very moment, he received strength to stand and say, "Unless someone can show me from these books and from Holy Scripture the error in my thinking, I will not and cannot recant. Here I stand. I can do no other, God help me!" And though he was condemned as an heretic, it was then that the torch of the Reformation began to spread throughout all of Europe. Nothing could stop the shining forth of the light.

Strength is what prayer provides, and that is what Gethsemane teaches. Jesus prayed when the flesh quailed. And though he sweat drops of blood, he stood firm and did the will of the Father. Peter slept. When the flesh was bold and confident, Peter slept. And the results follow in verses 43–50:

> And immediately, while he was still speaking, Judas came, one of the twelve, and with him a crowd with swords and clubs, from the chief priests and the scribes and the elders. Now the betrayer has given them a sign, saying, "The one I shall kiss is the man; seize him and lead him away safely." And when he came, he went up to him at once, and said, "Master!" And he kissed him. And they laid hands upon him and seized him. But one of those who stood by drew his sword, and struck the slave of the high priest and cut off his ear. And Jesus said to them, "Have you come out as against a robber, with swords and clubs to capture me? Day after day I was with you in the temple teach-

ing, and you did not seize me. But let the scriptures be fulfilled."
And they all forsook him, and fled (Mk. 14:43–50).

There are three actions emphasized in that paragraph. First,
the kiss of Judas. Mark uses the normal word for kiss, which
means "to love," in telling of the arrangement Judas had made
with the chief priests. They were to seize the one whom he
kissed. But in the actual moment, when Judas carries this out,
Mark uses an emphasized form of that word, a word that
means a prolonged kiss, a lover's kiss. I do not think there is
anything in all the annals of treachery more contemptuous
than this kiss of Judas—a deliberate, prolonged, apparently
loving act, done with cold determination to accomplish his
own purpose.

The second emphasis in this paragraph is on Peter's blunder-
ing defense. Peter is still trying to make a show of carrying out
what he resolved. He grabs the sword and, as the priests and
soldiers move in on Jesus, he slashes away. But so poor is his
aim that all he does is lop off the ear of the high priest's
servant. That is such a beautiful example of the flesh at work!
We may strike out in our attempts to carry out our purposes,
but all we accomplish is the lopping-off of somebody's ear.
As I look back on more than twenty-five years of pastoral
ministry, I am sure that if the symbols of my actions were
visibly apparent, one could look back and find lopped-off ears
lying all over the place! They are symbols of my attempts to
do what I thought was right—but it was not of the Lord. We
have all done this. The glorious thing, Luke tells us, is that
Jesus reached out and touched that servant and healed his ear.
I am so grateful for the Lord's healing touch on the lopped-off
ears that I have been responsible for during my lifetime.

The third action emphasized in this passage is the sudden
flight of the disciples. They all forsook him. I am sure this
means that at that moment, after three and one-half years, all
their confidence that Jesus was indeed the Messiah suddenly

forsakes them. They see now that he is nothing but a man. His willingness to give himself over without any resistance into the hands of his enemies and his refusal to defend himself in any way becomes, in their eyes, tantamount to his renunciation of being the Messiah. Now it is every man for himself, and so they flee.

In Luke's account of the resurrection, remember that as two disciples walked along the road to Emmaus, a stranger appeared—a man whom they did not recognize—and they discussed with him the events that had taken place in Jerusalem. They said to him, concerning Jesus of Nazareth, "We had hoped (notice the past tense) that he was the one who would redeem Israel." Their hope was gone, so they forsook him and fled. And, thus, the smiting of the Shepherd resulted in the scattering of the sheep.

Mark adds a little postscript in verse 51 that we do not want to miss: "And a young man followed him, with nothing but a linen cloth about his body; and they seized him, but he left the linen cloth and ran away naked." All the scholars agree that this is Mark himself. This is Mark's way of saying, "I was there." I am sure there are two things at least that he is telling us by this little account of his presence there. It is my conviction, derived from the *Stedmaniac* version of Scripture, that Mark himself was the rich young ruler who came to Jesus and asked the way to eternal life. Jesus said to him, "Go, sell what you have . . . and follow me," and that young man went away sad, because he had great possessions. I think there is some evidence that this was Mark. I believe this incident toward the end of the book is Mark's way of saying. "I did it. I went away and sold all that I had and gave it to the poor. All I had left was a robe. That night I followed him, and in the confusion and abruptness of the arrest, they laid hands on me and I lost even the robe!" And he fled away naked into the night.

It is also Mark's way of explaining to us how we got the

account of Gethsemane. None of the disciples could have given it. Eight of them were in a part of the garden some distance from Jesus. Three of them were close to him, but they were sound asleep and could not have heard the crying and the prayers; they did not see the angel come and minister to him. But somebody was watching. A certain young man was there watching the whole thing and gave us the story that we might have hope in the hour of our Gethsemane. This account can help us when we feel that we do not want to do what God tells us to do and we are confident that somehow we can work it out in our own strength. In that hour, we have Mark's account to remind us that we can come to a throne of grace and find mercy and grace to help in time of need.

# 13

# Jesus and the Priests

To some of us, events that occurred 2,000 years ago and so far away may seem rather remote from our own experience. Sometimes we are so caught up in our daily lives that these events seem rather dull because of their familiarity, especially in contrast to the exciting events that are happening all around us in today's world. But all these current events will be nothing but a dim memory ten years from now. Just think back to the things that were happening ten years ago and how unimportant they seem to us now.

But the events around the death of Jesus are the most significant events in all history—already every person in all the world who ever lived has been affected by these events. If we believe the Scriptures, this event is the focal point of history, not only on this planet but on every galaxy, every star, every solar system, every planet in all the vast reaches of space. These are the most crucial events that have ever taken place. It is, therefore, very important that we carefully study what has been recorded about them.

After Jesus was captured in Gethsemane Garden, he was

led away by the soldiers to the high priest. Mark doesn't record for us the appearance of Jesus before Annas, the father-in-law of the high priest, but he moves directly to the court-yard of Caiaphas, the current high priest:

> And they led Jesus to the high priest; and all the chief priests and the elders and the scribes were assembled. And Peter had followed him at a distance, right into the courtyard of the high priest; and he was sitting with the guards, and warming himself at the fire (Mk. 14:53–54).

Notice the very careful way Mark sets this scene for us. Jesus is in the inner room with the Sanhedrin. This assembly consisted of the high priest, all the chief priests, the scribes, and the elders—70 members of the Sanhedrin plus their help-ers and advisors. So it was a considerable crowd that gathered in the inner room in the residence of Caiaphas. There was Jesus in the midst of the Sanhedrin, while just outside in the outer courtyard where he could look in and see all that was happening, Peter sat with the guards around the fire on that chill spring night in Jerusalem. Mark is very careful to point out that these two situations occur side by side. As we look at this account very carefully, we will see why Mark contrasts these two situations. The trial before the priest proceeds in two stages. First, there is the testimony of the witnesses:

> Now the chief priests and the whole council sought testimony against Jesus to put him to death; but they found none. For many bore false witness against him, and their witness did not agree. And some stood up and bore false witness against him, saying, "We heard him say, 'I will destroy this temple that is made with hands, and in three days I will build another, not made with hands.' " Yet not even so did their testimony agree (Mk. 14: 55–59).

This trial is clearly a farce, with the outcome having been determined long before it was convened. Mark records that the

chief priests sought for testimony because they were determined to put Jesus to death. This reminds me of those accounts
of the early western vigilantes who announced to their victims
that they would be sure to give them a fair trial and then
hang them. This is what the chief priests did to Jesus.

The trial was illegal right from the very beginning. First,
it was held at night, and Jewish law insisted that all trials
before the priests be held in the daytime. Second, it met in
the wrong place. The Sanhedrin was to meet only in the hall
set aside for that purpose, and only meetings held there were
valid. But this meeting was held in the residence of the high
priest. Third, the Sanhedrin was prohibited by law from reaching a verdict on the same day that the trial was held, and here
the verdict is passed immediately at the end of this farcical
trial. Yet, despite all this connivance, including contrived testimony, things are not going well for the priests. Mark tells us
that although many bore false witness against him, the witnesses did not agree. As these witnesses one by one recounted
the very same events, there was such a discrepancy in their testi-
monies that it was obvious they were either telling a lie or
had not been there.

## An Element of Truth

These were the best witnesses money could buy, and yet
everything was falling apart and the priests were getting un-
easy and restless. But, finally, two men stood up—Matthew
tells us it was two who partially agreed. They said, "We heard
him say, 'I will destroy this temple that is made with hands,
and in three days I will build another, not made with hands.' "
Now that was the closest any of the witnesses had come to
agreeing. It was the strongest point in the case against Jesus,
for there was an element of truth in it. Early in Jesus' ministry,
when he first cleansed the temple, three and a half years before these events, he had said to the Jews, "Destroy this temple,
and in three days I will raise it up" (John 2:19). He meant,

"If you destroy this temple, then in three days, I will build it up again." He was pointing out the sharp contrast between their destructive efforts and his constructive powers. But John tells us that he was talking not about the temple of stone and brick, but of his own body; this was an early reference to the resurrection. He had not said, "I will destroy this temple," as these witnesses testified. Yet there was a germ of truth to what they said. Tennyson said, "A lie that is wholly a lie can be met and fought with outright, but a lie that is partly the truth is a harder matter to fight." These witnesses had enough truth to make something stick, but even then, Mark said, they couldn't agree in their details. So the case was falling apart, and the priests, I am sure, were feeling frustrated at this point, for it began to look as if they would not be able to find a legal ground by which to accomplish the murder of Jesus.

## Jesus Under Oath

At this point, the high priest saved the occasion, from the Sanhedrin's point of view:

> And the high priest stood up in the midst, and asked Jesus, "Have you no answer to make? What is it that these men testify against you?" But he was silent and made no answer (Mk. 14:60–61).

Isaiah had prophesied: "As a sheep before her shearers is dumb, so he opened not his mouth." Evidently our Lord understood that the testimony against him was so fragmentary, so weak, that it required no answer. He made no effort to defend himself or to answer the lies of the witnesses, but he remained silent. The high priest was stunned by Jesus' silence, and so he did something absolutely illegal; he put Jesus under oath to testify against himself.    *Matt. 26:63*

> Again the high priest asked him, "Are you the Christ, the Son of the Blessed?" And Jesus said, "I am; and you will see the Son

of man sitting at the right hand of Power, and coming with the clouds of heaven." And the high priest tore his mantle, and said, "Why do we still need witnesses? You have heard his blasphemy. What is your decision?" And they all condemned him as deserving death. And some began to spit on him, and to cover his face, and to strike him, saying to him, "Prophesy!" And the guards received him with blows (Mk. 14:61–65).

Matthew says that the high priest put Jesus under oath. He said to him, "I adjure you by the living God . . ." This was a very solemn oath, and Jesus breaks his silence and answers the high priest's question: "Are you the Messiah, the Son of the Blessed One?" Now what the priest is really asking is, "Are you the one whom the Old Testament predicts will come, the Messiah, the Promised One? Are you the Son of God?" Jesus responds very simply, "I am."

There are many critics and liberal scholars of the New Testament who insist that at no time did Jesus ever claim to be the Messiah or the Son of God. They tell us that these claims were made about him by his disciples. If you ever hear anyone say that, just turn to this passage of Scripture. There are other places where Jesus clearly claims to be the Messiah and the Son of God, but this one is the clearest because he was under solemn oath to tell the truth, and he simply and clearly states, "I am the Messiah—I am the Son of God." There is no doubt about it.

The rest of his reply is directed to the high priest personally, for he says to him, "And you will see the Son of man sitting at the right hand of Power, and coming with the clouds of heaven." In saying this to Caiaphas, Jesus is informing him of his own destiny.

We know from other Scriptures that when people die, whether they are believers or unbelievers, they step out of time into eternity. Events that are long distant yet in time, are suddenly present in eternity. The Scriptures reveal that the event for which believers are being prepared and are waiting for here on earth is the coming of the Lord with thousands of his saints for his own. I believe that this explains why oftentimes when believers die, in the last moment of life, they break out in a big smile and a look of expectation comes into their eyes. Sometimes they will even cry out because what they are seeing is the Lord coming with his saints for his own.

Unbelievers, too, step out of time into eternity when they die, and the event which they see is what Jesus describes here. "You will see the Son of man sitting at the right hand of Power, and coming . . ." as a judge upon the earth. They see him as the judge. They see the great white throne, the impressive scene described in Revelation 20 when all the dead are gathered together and the books are open and men stand before the judge of all the earth. To this high priest in his arrogant unbelief, Jesus says, "Now you are the judge, I am the prisoner; one day I will be the judge, you will be the prisoner." With this he answers the blasphemous unbelief of this high priest.

The high priest, in a hypocritical gesture, tears his garments when he hears Jesus' claim to be the Messiah. He rends his garments indicating supposed outrage at Jesus' statement. This is hypocritical because Jesus had said exactly what Caiaphas wanted him to say. He knew that when Jesus made a claim like that in the presence of the Sanhedrin, his doom was sealed. And so the priest by this hypocritical act indicates a phony outrage and demands the verdict, and the Sanhedrin immediately passes the sentence and condemns Jesus to death.

## Hatred Unleashed

Then a strange thing happens. Mark tells us that upon the passing of the verdict all forces of restraint that had been upon these priests and scribes and elders seemed to be lifted, and they again committed a wholly illegal act. They began to vent their hatred upon Jesus and pour out in venomous abuse all the pent-up jealousy and hatred they had stored up against him. They began to spit on him, which is the ultimate insult, and to beat him. They covered his face with a garment, and while his face was hidden, they hit him and said, "Prophesy! Tell us who hit you." Thus they mocked him and scorned him and insulted him. Seven hundred and fifty years before this Isaiah had spoken the words that Jesus must indeed have been thinking: "I gave my back to the smiter and my cheeks to those who plucked out the hair. I hid not my face from shame and spitting."

Outside, Peter was watching this, and he never forgot it. In his first letter he tells us that we are to remember that scene and take heed to it, for Christ was our example. "When he was reviled, he did not revile in return; when he suffered, he did not threaten; but he trusted to him who judges justly" (1 Pet. 2:23). This is how Christians are to respond when they are falsely accused, when they are unjustly vilified and abused. Instead of retorting and trying to justify ourselves, Peter says, we are to return good for evil, revile not in return, but commit ourselves to him who is able to judge things justly —God himself.

Now Mark takes us to Peter, outside the court:

> And as Peter was below in the courtyard, one of the maids of the high priest came; and seeing Peter warming himself, she looked at him, and said, "You also were with the Nazarene, Jesus." But he denied it, saying, "I neither know nor understand what you mean." And he went out into the gateway. And the maid saw him, and began again to say to the bystanders, "This man is one of them." But again he denied it. And after a little while again the bystanders said to Peter, "Certainly you are one of them; for you are a Galilean." But he began to invoke a curse on himself and to swear, "I do not know this man of whom you speak." And immediately the cock crowed a second time. And Peter remembered how Jesus had said to him, "Before the cock crows twice, you will deny me three times." And he broke down and wept (Mk. 14:66–72).

Peter's determination to show himself faithful to Christ has carried him right into the courtyard of the high priest where he is warming his hands around the fire with the very guards who had arrested Jesus and brought him there. That was a brave thing to do; he was in terrible danger. I think it was the pride of Peter's heart that brought him this far. He was so determined not to let the Lord down, so determined to show that Jesus was wrong when he said Peter would deny him. But now that he is there in the midst of the enemies of Jesus fears begin to possess his heart, and the bravado melts away— his courage is gone.

## Pesky Maid

The young woman who had let him in the door, a servant of the high priest, recognized him and said, "You are one of the Nazarene's followers, aren't you?" John, writing years later, tells us that there was another disciple present. Many of the commentators think it was John himself, but I think it was Mark. If Mark was the rich young ruler, he would fit John's description of a disciple who was known to the high priest and who had spoken to this maid to let Peter into the courtyard. Therefore, when Peter came in and the maid saw that a man whom she knew to be a disciple had let him in, she was sure that this was also one of the disciples, and so she accused him of it.

Right away, Peter's defenses have gone. He says immediately, "I don't know who you are talking about." He tries to turn off this inquisitive maid. Leaving the fireside, he goes outside to the gateway so he will be less visible. But the pesky girl follows him and keeps pursuing the subject, much to the discomfort and embarrassment of Peter. The maid says to the people standing around, "This man is one of them." I'm sure Peter could have choked her gladly. But she kept pursuing him. As he protested, they heard his accent. Peter was as outstanding in that crowd as a Texan in Peoria. His accent gave him away. So the people said, "You must be one of them; you're from Galilee." Once again, Peter denied it vehemently. It says he cursed. Now that doesn't mean he began to blaspheme and swear. It means that he pronounced a curse upon himself. He said, "God curse me if what I say is not the truth." He took a solemn oath.

I think Mark is careful to point out the contrast between Jesus speaking under oath in the inner courtroom and Peter's oath in the courtyard outside. Jesus said he was the Messiah, the Son of God, and Peter denied that he knew Jesus at all. That was a solemn and very serious oath, and just then, Mark says, "the cock crowed a second time." Peter's conscience smote him. He knew what he had done, and according to the account here, he broke down and wept. The word for "broke down" is very strong in Greek. He literally went out and threw himself down on the ground in agony and tears of repentance and remorse began to flow as he thought of what he had done.

Nothing intrigues me more in the Gospels than to see the careful way the writers choose incidents that belong together, placing them side by side to reveal truth that we might otherwise never see. One reason Mark has done that here is so we might see the contrast. Here is a band of priests who hate Jesus. Their hearts are filled with venom and anger and jealousy and bitterness against him. And all of it comes spilling out in the spitting and buffeting that follows the verdict. Contrasted to this is a man who loves Jesus with all his heart and is determined to defend him to the end. And yet, in the moment of crisis he fails Jesus, he denies that he even knows him.

But the most important reason Mark put these two situations side by side is so that we might understand that both of them manifest the same thing; both are a manifestation of the undependability of human nature—the flesh, as the Bible calls it. These priests were men of the flesh, men who lived according to the ways of the world, men who thought as the world thinks and who were seeking for status and prestige and position. Jesus was a threat to their position and awakened their hatred and their anger, which they expressed in this terrible accusation and mockery and violence against Jesus. That is the flesh at work. Everybody recognizes that hatred and anger and vehemence are wrong, and we know those things come from an evil, perverted heart. But what Mark wants us to see is that the love of Peter was no better. Peter was also depending on the flesh—on human abilities and human resources—to carry him through. In the hour of crisis that kind of love was no more effective than the hatred of the priests. Love and loyalty and faithfulness mean nothing when they rest on the shaky foundation of the determination of a human will. Mark puts these two examples side by side so that we might see their similarities.

## The Hopeful Difference

To me, the most hopeful note here is the tears of Peter. The priests didn't weep, and there is no record that Judas wept, though he did display a degree of remorse and despair. But Peter, when he denied his Lord, threw himself down and wept. Somebody said to me recently that he had learned a lesson about failure; he had learned that failure is never the end of the story. This is true of Peter. Peter's tears speak of another day that is yet to come when the Lord will deliver him and restore him, having learned a very sobering and salutary lesson.

Remember the resurrection morning when Jesus met the women at the tomb. He said to them, "Go and tell my disciples and Peter—*and Peter*—that I go before them and will meet them in Galilee." After he denies Christ Peter drops out of the picture; we know nothing more about what happened to him until the women come with the good news of the resurrection. The only difference between the denial of Peter and the hatred of the priests was the tears that Peter shed. Those tears meant there was life that could be restored; his failure could be forgotten and forgiven.

When I look at Christianity today, I am sometimes appalled at the degree that we depend upon the flesh. I am amazed and intrigued as we look at the Scriptures to see that God always works in simplicity and with a low-keyed approach. God loves that. Our attempts, and the flesh's attempts, are almost always characterized by high gear, high promotion, and complexity. I learned long ago that when things start getting very complex, when you need finely tuned organizations to carry them out and hundreds of people—somehow you've missed it, for God's work is characterized by simplicity. Paul wrote in 2 Corinthians 11:3, "I am greatly concerned about you lest Satan should woo you from the simplicity that is in Christ." It is only by a sense of weakness that rests upon the power and wisdom of God that we can accomplish anything. When we do, we don't need high gear, high power machinery. We don't need expensive approaches. One of the things that turns me off about Christendom is to see how much of it depends upon the power of money. I believe that God never needs money, but he uses money. Money is always available when God is at work. But if a project depends on money and people are thinking in terms of money, they have missed the simplicity that is in Christ. May the Lord teach us from this simple story the utter undependability of the flesh and the constant victory and triumph of resting in the Spirit.

# 14

# Jesus and the Rulers

The fifteenth chapter of Mark's Gospel is the account of our Lord's appearance before Pilate. The events around the cross are more than simple narratives told by the Gospel writers. You can read them that way: the simple tragic story of a man who laid down his life on behalf of a cause. But if you read the Gospel accounts carefully, you will see that there are very strange and marvelous forces at work behind the scenes. We sometimes sing these words, "God moves in a mysterious way, His wonders to perform." I do not think anything makes that more clear than these Gospel accounts. The apostle Paul says, "But we impart a secret and hidden wisdom of God. . . . None of the rulers of this age understood this; for if they had, they would not have crucified the Lord of glory" (1 Cor. 2:7). So there is something going on behind the scenes in this account, and it has to do with the radical power of the cross in people's lives.

In chapter 14 Jesus appeared before the priests, and the issue was whether or not he was the prophet that was to come— the Messiah who would come from God to set things right within the nation. But the account before us now has to do with Jesus' appearance before Pilate, and the issue is, "Is he the King of the Jews?" That question is foremost throughout this portion of Scripture. Yet underneath are currents that indicate that something much deeper is going on, something of mystery. I would like you to be thinking of four questions as we read this account. The first one is: Why did Pilate marvel at the silence of Jesus? Second, why did the crowd choose Barabbas instead of Jesus? Third, why did Pilate scourge Jesus before his crucifixion? And fourth, why did the soldiers mock him with such passion and cruelty? As we seek to answer these questions, we will get at the story behind the story.

The first question is raised in chapter 15:

> And as soon as it was morning the chief priests, with the elders and scribes, and the whole council held a consultation, and they bound Jesus and led him away and delivered him to Pilate. And Pilate asked him, "Are you the King of the Jews?" And he answered him, "You have said so." And the chief priests accused him of many things. And Pilate again asked him, "Have you no answer to make? See how many charges they bring against you." But Jesus made no further answer, so that Pilate wondered (Mk. 15:1–5).

We do not know how our Lord spent the hours between his late evening appearance before the priests and his appearance here before Pilate the next morning. There were probably five or six hours in between. It is hard to say whether or not he was able to get a few hours' sleep after that momentous night when he had been betrayed and arrested and condemned. But early the next morning he is brought before them again, and the priests hold a consultation with the entire Sanhedrin. Since their meeting at night was illegal, in order to justify their actions, they have to hold a meeting in the daytime.

The reason for their early morning consultation was that they knew that the charge on which they had condemned Jesus would never stand before the Roman governor. They had condemned Jesus for blasphemy. They said that he claimed to be God, so he was worthy of death. But the Romans would pay no attention to that charge, so they had to come up with something else before they sent him to Pilate. Luke tells us that they levied three charges against him. First, he was charged with perverting the nation, that is, arousing troublemakers, creating riots and dissension. Second, he was charged with forbidding the payment of tribute to Rome, teaching people to not pay their taxes. Third, he was charged with wanting to be king instead of Caesar. It is this last charge that Pilate seized upon as being the only important one of the three, and he said to him, "Are you the King of the Jews?"

## No Threat to Rome

Jesus' answer has puzzled a lot of people. He did not say, as he had previously said to the priests, "I am." He said, "You have said so," or "So you say." Many have been troubled by that, for it is neither an affirmation nor a denial, but simply, "That is what you say. Am I the King of the Jews? According to your way of thinking, you would call me King of the Jews." Why was he not more positive? I think the answer is clear in John's Gospel where we read that Jesus went on to say, "My kingship is not of this world; if my kingship were of this world, my servants would fight . . " (John 18:36). He makes clear to Pilate that his kingship is no threat to Rome whatsoever. I think Pilate understood it that way and was relieved of any fear that Jesus was indeed trying to foment a revolution against Rome.

If we read between the lines here, we can see that the priests began to see that Pilate understood that Jesus was not challenging the authority of Rome and their case was beginning to fall apart. They were angry, Mark tells us, and began to accuse him of many things. They heaped on all the accusations they could think of to convince Pilate that this man should be put to death. In a very revealing comment in verse 10, Mark says that Pilate "perceived that it was out of envy that the chief priests had delivered him up." Now Pilate was no fool. He was a cruel and rapacious governor, but he was no fool. He saw through all these empty charges and understood what the priests were trying to do and why. Envy means a desire for something that someone else has. You are covetous of it; if you cannot have it yourself, you do not want the other person to have it either. What the priests wanted was Jesus' power and authority with the people. "He spoke as no other man spoke," and they knew that. Again and again they had tried to gainsay what he said and to trap him with his own words, but they could never catch him. He always had a word, a simple word, that utterly demolished them and all their schemes. Such craft and power made them angry and envious.

Now to all these additional charges that the priests heaped upon him, Jesus remained absolutely silent. He just stood there. Pilate was amazed at this and tried to encourage him to answer: "Have you no answer to make? See how many charges they bring against you." Once again the Lord stood without uttering a word. He did not even reply to Pilate. So it is recorded here that Pilate marveled at our Lord's silence. Why did Jesus remain silent and why was the governor so struck by this silence of Jesus?

## Sympathy with Jesus

If you read further in the chapter you find that some hours later, when Jesus was hanging on the cross, the chief priests and others were standing around, taunting him and mocking him.

And those who passed by derided him, wagging their heads and saying, "Aha! You who would destroy the temple and build it in three days, save yourself, and come down from the cross!" So also the chief priests mocked him to one another with the scribes, saying, "He saved others; he cannot save himself" (Mk. 15: 29–32).

When they made that statement, they were wrong. They thought that he could not save himself, but he could have. I think that here before Pilate it was quite possible for Jesus to save himself from the cross. For it was evident to him that Pilate knew he was innocent and wanted to deliver him and was seeking some way to do so. If he had replied to Pilate in any way, the governor would have used his words to dismiss the charge and free him immediately. It is obvious that Pilate's sympathy at this point is with Jesus, not with the priests. He knows what they are trying to do, that they are trying to rail-road Jesus. He knows that the man is innocent and is no real threat to Rome, and he wants to set him free. But he marveled because Jesus would not cooperate. He did not say a word, and gave Pilate no grounds on which to free him. Thus, the silence of Jesus effectively exposed the true enmity of these priests. It stripped away all their disguise, and they had to come out and openly reveal that what was eating them was nothing more than the jealousy of their own hearts.

That is what I mean when I say the cross has a remarkable way of working with us. It strips us of all pretense. It is God's great plowshare, ripping through the hypocrisy of our lives and laying us bare for all to see, including ourselves. This is what you see happening here. As Jesus remains silent before these priests, they are forced to make clear the enmity of their own hearts against him.

The second movement of this story begins in the incident with Barabbas. The other Gospel accounts tell us that at this point Pilate sent Jesus to Herod. Herod, who was considered king of the Jews, tried to make sport of Jesus and asked him to work a miracle. But Jesus remained utterly silent before Herod. So Herod sent him back to Pilate, and here Mark takes up the narrative in verse 6:

> Now at the feast he used to release for them one prisoner whom they asked. And among the rebels in prison, who had committed murder in the insurrection, there was a man called Barabbas. And the crowd came up and began to ask Pilate to do as he was wont to do for them. And he answered them, "Do you want me to release for you the King of the Jews?" For he perceived that it was out of envy that the chief priests had delivered him up. But the chief priests stirred up the crowd to have him release for them Barabbas instead. And Pilate again said to them, "Then what shall I do with the man whom you call the King of the Jews?" And they cried out again, "Crucify him." And Pilate said to them, "Why, what evil has he done?" But they shouted all the more, "Crucify him." So Pilate, wishing to satisfy the crowd, released for them Barabbas; and having scourged Jesus, he delivered him to be crucified (Mk. 15:6-15).

All the Gospel writers tell us of Barabbas. He was a bloodthirsty revolutionary, a member of the first-century edition of the Symbionese Liberation Army; hard-nosed, bloody-handed, a murderer, as Luke tells us. The interesting thing about him is his name, which means "son of the father." In a most dramatic historic coincidence, according to some old manuscripts, there is some evidence that his name probably was Jesus Barabbas: Jesus, son of the father. This is again God's subtle teaching: that "hidden and secret wisdom of God" Paul speaks of that as silently guiding events behind the scene, bringing things to light that otherwise would never be known. For this crowd is now confronted with choosing between Jesus, the son of the father, who rules by force and makes his living by his wits; and Jesus, the son of the Father, who rules by love and is ready to sacrifice himself.

## Disappointed with Jesus

Now I think we have to ask why they chose Barabbas. The answer seems to be that they were disappointed with Jesus. This was the crowd which, just a few days before, had welcomed him into Jerusalem. The city was filled with people Jesus had healed. The eyes of the blind had been opened, the deaf made to hear, and the lame to walk. There must have been hundreds and probably thousands of people in Jerusalem at that time whom Jesus had touched personally. He had awakened within the people the hope, the flaming desire, that this was indeed the Messiah come to deliver them from the yoke of Rome. All their ideas of messiahship centered around the thought that he would be the one who would set them free from the hated bondage of Rome. Now, when they saw him standing helpless before the Roman governor, saw his apparent unwillingness or inability to make any defense, or to get out of this by any means, or to do anything against the Romans, all their loyalty to him collapsed. In anger and disappointment, they turned and chose Jesus, the son of the father, who lived by force—Barabbas the murderer.

We, too, face the same decision these Jews had to make between Barabbas and Jesus. Have you ever been disappointed in Jesus, disappointed in God? Have you ever expected him to act in a certain way because of what you understood about him and his life and his nature—but he did not do it. Has that ever happened to you? It has to me. I have been angry and disappointed in God. I have been all but convinced that he did not live up to his promise, for I was sure that I knew what he was going to do, and God disappointed me. My heart was filled with rage that God would act that way, despite the fact that God has told us all, again and again, "My ways are not your ways, and my thoughts are not your thoughts. As the heavens are higher than the earth, so are my ways higher than your ways, and my thoughts higher than your thoughts." We cannot figure God out. He will be true to himself, he will never lie, he will never deceive us; but he is more than we can handle. He is bigger than we are. And, like this crowd, when we get angry with God and upset with Jesus and turn from him, there is always another Jesus waiting in the wings for us to follow.

The scourging of Jesus related in this paragraph raises another question. Pilate knew that the crowd wanted him to release Barabbas and not Jesus. He asked them, "What shall I do then with Jesus, the King of the Jews?" And they said, "Crucify him." I think Pilate was somewhat aghast at that. There was no basis for him to order Jesus to be crucified, and yet the crowd was demanding it. Pilate was a manpleaser, so he scourged Jesus. Now it was not the normal practice to scourge a prisoner before crucifying him. There is no evidence that the other thieves who were crucified with Jesus were scourged before they went to the cross. But Pilate ordered Jesus to be scourged.

If you have seen what the Romans used in this process of scourging, you realize what a bloody and bitter experience it was. These long leather cords were imbedded with bits of metal and bone, so that as the thongs whipped around him, the skin on the prisoner's back was cut and flayed open until it was a bloody mass. I have often wondered why it was that Pilate ordered this scourging, knowing that crucifixion would follow. But I think it is clear that this was the last attempt by Pilate to spare Jesus. He hoped by the scourging to awaken the sympathy of the crowd. He hoped to punish him in a way that would arouse the feeling of the crowd on his behalf. For John tells us that after the scourging Pilate led Jesus out before the crowd and said to them, "Behold the man!" But it failed. Stirred up by the chief priests and others, the crowd kept crying in their madness, "Crucify him!"

John tells us that Pilate was afraid of Jesus, and here we can see that he was afraid of the crowd. So as this account unfolds, you see a man of dubious character caught on the horns of a dilemma. Trying to please two opposing powers, he is stripped naked before all of history, and we begin to see this man in his true character. He is a coward, afraid to make the decision on the basis of justice. Instead, he decides on the basis of expediency, and he ends up the curse of all the ages. See how the cross again is at work behind the scenes, bringing out the hidden things.

## Strange Mockery

Now the final paragraph deals with the soldiers:

And the soldiers led him away inside the palace (that is, the praetorium); and they called together the whole battalion. And they clothed him in a purple cloak, and plaiting a crown of thorns they put it on him. And they began to salute him, "Hail, King of the Jews!" And they struck his head with a reed, and spat upon him, and they knelt down in homage to him. And when they had mocked him, they stripped him of the purple cloak, and put his own clothes on him. And they led him out to crucify him (Mk. 15:16–20).

This mockery was a strange thing. They did not usually do this with those sentenced to crucifixion. These were rough, hard-handed soldiers, accustomed to carrying out gruesome orders. They could take a man out and nail him to a cross and then go in to breakfast. But this mockery of Jesus seems to have a tremendous passion behind it. Notice they called the whole band together, all the soldiers who were off duty or lounging around; they were all joined together in this. It was spontaneous. They did not have to do this; they suddenly decided on their own to indulge in this cruel mockery. They made the crown of thorns and jammed it down on the Lord's head; they put a reed in his hand as his scepter and bowed down before him; they spit on him and jerked the reed out of his hand and hit him over the head with it.

Why this strange mockery? I think the answer is revealed in what they said to him: "Hail, King of the Jews!" They were not angry at Jesus. They probably had never seen him before and knew very little about him. But they were angry at the Jews. All the pent-up hatred and resentment against this stubborn and difficult people came pouring out and found its object in this lonely Jew whom they understood was regarded in some sense as King of the Jews. All the foul mass of bigotry and racial hatred came pouring out against Jesus. Once again we see how the cross unveils what is hidden. The second psalm begins with these words:

Why do the nations conspire, and the peoples plot in vain? The kings of the earth set themselves, and the rulers take counsel together, against the Lord and his anointed, saying, "Let us burst their bonds asunder, and cast their cords from us" (Ps. 2:1–3).

As you read through this account you can see that God is subtly moving in strange and various ways behind the scenes to answer the question asked by the Psalmist. As the cross of Jesus comes into the life of any man, woman, boy, or girl, it has a powerful way of ripping off all our disguise, and we have to answer finally, clearly, and honestly what our reaction is to Jesus.

That is why the great question of all time is, "What will you do with Jesus, who is called the Christ?" What is your attitude toward Jesus? Do you love him? Paul writes, "Any one who does not love the Lord Jesus Christ, let him be accursed." The word is, "let him be damned." Now why would he say a harsh thing like that? Because that is the test. If you do not love Jesus, what do you love? You love the opposite. Instead of loving love, you love hate. Instead of loving truth, you love lies. Instead of loving honesty, you love deceit. It is the final testing of all time and of every person. What do you feel about Jesus? Do you love him? Most of us do. But even in those hours when we act differently, the cross has this strange and marvelous way of penetrating deep beneath the surface and bringing out all that hidden secret wisdom of God which none of the rulers of this age understand; for if they had, they never would have crucified the Lord of glory. Every one of us finally stands naked before God. I hope that if your attitude is anything other than a love for Jesus, you will surrender that attitude to him. You cannot change your heart, but he can. If you bring it to him, he will make the change.

# 15

# The Awful Penalty

Mark 15 brings us to the account of the crucifixion. Because of the sacredness of this incident, will you pray with me for a moment before we look into this passage?

Our Father, we ask that your Holy Spirit may take the scene that we look at now and imprint it deeply upon our own hearts and minds, and that we may understand something of the marvelous implications of it. We know that we are not looking at a mere martyrdom of a man of high ideals, but we are looking at the payment of a ransom for sin. We pray that we may understand it and that the eyes of our hearts may be enlightened that we may grasp this truth as it pertains to each of us. In Jesus' name, Amen.

Mark's account of the crucifixion is somewhat different from that of the other Gospel writers. Mark leaves out a great many things that the others have included. For instance, Mark includes only one sentence out of the seven spoken by Jesus from the cross. In fact, the actual description of Jesus' actions and words that Mark records are limited to three very short

passages in this account. You will find the first of these in
Mark 15:22: "And they brought him to the place called
Golgotha (which means the place of a skull)."

Right outside the Damascus gate in the northern wall of
Jerusalem is a little mount that looks like a skull, and many
feel that this is the place where Jesus was crucified. It was
called in Hebrew "Golgotha," which means skull. Then Mark
says, "And they offered him wine mingled with myrrh; but he
did not take it" (Mk. 15:23).

This is man's feeble attempt to allay the pain and the suffering of the cross, "but he did not take it." Then Mark says,
in just four short words, "And they crucified him."

The Gospel writers show a tremendous reserve about describing the crucifixion. None of them describes the driving
of the nails or the agony of Jesus; it is simply put in these
stark terms, "And they crucified him." Mark skips over almost
all of the first three hours on the cross to the ninth hour, when
Jesus cries out:

> And when the sixth hour had come, there was darkness over
> the whole land until the ninth hour. And at the ninth hour Jesus
> cried with a loud voice, "Elo-i, Elo-i, lama sabach-thani?" which
> means, "My God, my God, why hast thou forsaken me?" (Mk.
> 15:33).

The third and final passage of description that Mark gives
is in verse 37: "And Jesus uttered a loud cry, and breathed
his last. And the curtain of the temple was torn in two, from
top to bottom."

The rest of the account in the Gospel of Mark focuses on the
people gathered around the cross. Mark's view is not the view
of the crowd looking at Jesus, but it is rather the view from
the cross itself, looking at the crowd. Gathered around the
foot of the cross were a great number of individuals or groups
of individuals whom he brings before us so that we might see
their reactions to the crucifixion of our Lord.

Mark clearly intended this to be a contrast between the in-
scrutable workings of God and the ways and the thinking of
man. What he is saying to us is that this event is timeless.
If Jesus were crucified today, these same people would be
gathered around the cross; the cast of characters would remain
unchanged. No matter what time or age the scene of Calvary
was enacted for us, these same attitudes would always be dis-
played. I think that is the purpose of Mark's careful, deliberate
descriptions of those who gathered around the cross.

### Unwilling Involvement

The first of these character descriptions is found in verse 21
where Mark describes an incident that occurred as Jesus was
on his way to the cross. The Roman soldiers have been com-
missioned to take Jesus out to crucify him. On the way from
Pilate's judgment seat, as they are going down the Via
Dolorosa, the "way of sorrows," through the streets of Jerusalem, Jesus stumbles and falls. When he stumbles a second time,
the Roman soldiers grab a stranger in the crowd and impress
him to bear the cross of Jesus: "And they compelled a
passer-by, Simon of Cyrene, who was coming in from the
country, the father of Alexander and Rufus, to carry his cross"
(Mk. 15:21).

Just picture the feelings and attitudes of Simon when he was
thus so rudely interrupted in what he had scheduled to do
that day. He was from the country of Cyrene in North Africa
and had come to Jerusalem to celebrate the passover feast. He
was coming from his lodgings outside the city and had no idea
that this strange event was about to take place. But as he was
watching Jesus stagger under the weight of the cross, Simon
suddenly was grabbed by the soldiers and forced to carry the
cross. There is little question that his feeling was one of anger
at this interruption. Undoubtedly, his attitude was one of unwilling involvement.

This is a common attitude of many today toward God and

the things of God, especially toward the cross. Many people are resentful that God should ever change their plans—should ever interrupt what they have scheduled to happen. I have felt this way myself, and so have you. We resent it when some circumstance over which we have no control suddenly changes our plans, especially if it involves pain and suffering. This was the attitude of Simon of Cyrene as he bore the cross of Jesus.

There is much evidence in the Scripture that this event had a tremendous effect on Simon's life. There is a hint in the book of Acts that Simon was there on the Day of Pentecost and very likely did become a Christian as a result of this sudden interruption of his plans. Mark tells us that Simon was the father of Alexander and Rufus, who are apparently well-known to the gentile believers to whom Mark is writing. In chapter 16 of Paul's letter to the Romans, he mentions a Rufus with whom he was very closely associated and whose mother had been kind to Paul. It may well be the same Rufus. But here Mark simply brings out Simon's attitude of unwilling involvement in the crucifixion of Jesus.

Gathered around the foot of the cross itself were the soldiers who had crucified Jesus, those rough Roman soldiers who had crucified perhaps scores and scores of people. This was a time of great unrest and trouble in the land of Israel and there were others who were crucified about this time. Undoubtedly, these soldiers had much experience in crucifixion, because when they had finished their work and Jesus was hanging from the cross, these callous soldiers got out a pair of dice and started a crap game at the foot of the cross. It seems strange to us that any man could contemplate the dying of Jesus and carry on in such a way. But here were men who were far more interested in making a buck than they were in the blood of Jesus. Mark indicates by this that in all times there are many people who are not at all concerned about the meaning of the death of Christ. Their whole concern is focused on making a fast buck. These soldiers stand forever as examples of those callous individuals who have no interest in the great story of the cross—who shrug their shoulders with careless indifference to anybody who tries to call their attention to what was really happening at this scene. They just go back to their money-grubbing habits.

## Angry Young Men

Also associated with the cross were the robbers who were crucified with Jesus: "And with him they crucified two robbers, one on his right and one on his left" (Mk. 15:27). And later, Mark adds: "Those who were crucified with him also reviled him" (Mk. 15:32).

Here are two men who had been arrested in their campaign of terror and violence; they were professional revolutionaries. They were angry young men, committed to the philosophy of "get what you can any way that you can and it doesn't matter who is hurt in the process." These two looked upon Jesus as the same kind of man; they took out all their frustrations on him and reviled him because he could be of no more help to them than they could be to him.

Mark doesn't tell us what happened to one of these men. Other Gospel writers inform us that the other was watching all that was happening and repented of his abuse of Jesus. He said, "We deserve to be here, but this man does not deserve this." One of the most beautiful things about the story of the crucifixion is that just before Jesus breathed his last, this man, seeing all that had happened, suddenly realized in a moment of truth that Jesus was indeed a king entering a kingdom in which he had great power and authority. This one-time robber threw himself on the mercy of Jesus an. cried out in a voice that has echoed through the centuries, "Lord, remember me when you come into your kingdom."

In verse 29, Mark also tells us that there were certain passers-by who came by the cross as Jesus was suspended on it.

> And those who passed by derided him, wagging their heads, and saying, "Aha! You who would destroy the temple and build it in three days, save yourself, and come down from the cross!" (Mk. 15:29).

These were just bystanders, but when they saw Jesus, they remembered that he was the one who had made these great claims, and they said, "Look, they've caught you, haven't they? You've gone too far. You were doing fine teaching the people, but then you began making these ridiculous claims that you could destroy the temple and raise it up again. You got what you had coming." Notice that Mark shows the derision by the little phrase: they went by "wagging their heads and saying, 'Aha!' " They heaped abuse on him.

There are many people today who feel that way. There are groups of people who make a great deal over the teachings of Jesus. Some even advertise themselves as following him as the great moral leader and teacher. They are widely spreading the idea that the teachings of Jesus are designed to bless man. But whenever these people read in the Scriptures any claim by Jesus that he is anything more than human, whenever they see that he made any claims to the supernatural or said, "I am the Son of God," or "I am the only way to the Father," they can't accept it. They cannot buy that kind of a claim and they rip it out of their Bibles. Mark makes it clear that such a view of the person of Jesus is dead wrong and stops short of an acknowledgement that would lead to the realization of what God wants them to see in him.

In verses 31–32, Mark describes the priests who also were at the cross:

> So also the chief priests mocked him to one another with the scribes, saying, "He saved others; he cannot save himself. Let the Christ, the King of Israel, come down now from the cross, that we may see and believe" (Mk. 15:31–32).

These priests had been very frightened of Jesus before, but now they have become arrogant. Before, they were threatened by him. They saw that he was able to lead and teach the crowds and bless them in ways that the priests had no power to do themselves. So they were jealous of him and angry at him, and they accomplished his death. Now their moment had come, and they stood around the cross mocking him and gloating over his helplessness. They threw at him these words, "Come down from the cross and save yourself; you've saved others, but you can't save yourself. If you'll just come down from the cross, we'll see and believe." There are many religious leaders today who use the name of Christianity but say they can accept everything about Christianity except the cross. If Jesus would just abandon the cross, they could swallow the whole thing. They don't like the cross because of the gore and the blood. If you ever hear a gospel preached that doesn't have at its core the cross of Jesus Christ, then you are listening to what Paul called "another gospel," which is anathema to God. The cross is at the very heart of the good news of Jesus Christ.

## Curiosity on a Sponge

There was another fellow at the cross who was interested in all the proceedings. His name is not given to us; he was just one of the bystanders. But he enters the picture when Jesus calls out to God:

> And some of the bystanders hearing it said, "Behold, he is calling Elijah." And one ran and, filling a sponge full of vinegar, put it on a reed and gave it to him to drink, saying, "Wait, let us see whether Elijah will come to take him down" (Mk. 15:35–36).

At first glance it looks as if this man is moved with compassion for Jesus. He runs to get vinegar, an anesthetic that will deaden the pain of suffering, and fills a sponge with it and puts it up to the lips of Jesus. It looks as though he is trying to relieve his suffering by offering him some relief. But if you look at Mark's account carefully, that is not his motive at all. His motive is to see if something exciting will happen. He is not moved by compassion, but by curiosity.

Sometimes you read in the papers about a man who has

crawled out on a ledge over a city street and is about to commit suicide. A crowd gathers below to watch him. Perhaps he will sit there in indecision for moments, even hours; but the crowd keeps waiting to see when he will jump. As he delays, they become impatient and some of them yell up at him, "Jump, what's the matter?" It is indicative of the thrill-seeking desires of people today who would have their own momentary passions met at the cost of a human life. This man at the cross is saying, "Let's delay this death." He gave Jesus the sponge so he would not die too quickly. "Wait," he said. "Let's see whether Elijah will come and deliver him." I think perhaps of all those who gathered around the cross of Christ, there is no incident more characteristic of our own day than the cheap, thrill-seeking desire for pleasure that this man exhibits.

At this point, Jesus dies. He calls out with a loud cry and breathes his last. Mark still has three more accounts about the people who gathered around the cross, but these people are of a different character. After the death of Jesus, there is no mention of anybody who abused, mocked, or reviled him. Those described now are the lovers and admirers of Jesus. The first, found in Mk. 15:39, is the centurion who was in charge of the crucifixion crew. "And when the centurion, who stood facing him, saw that he thus breathed his last, he said, 'Truly this man was the Son of God.'"

This centurion was a pagan; he probably believed in many gods. Yet the cross brought him to a sobering awareness of the reality that what he was watching was not a joke after all— that some ghastly mistake was being made in the crucifixion of this man. He sees that Jesus indeed is a royal personage, the Son of God, and this centurion, perhaps used to appearing in the presence of royalty, suddenly becomes aware of the true character of Jesus. Notice he speaks in the past tense—this man *was* the Son of God. There is no hope here; there is no understanding that there may be help for him in the process.

I think this is representative of many people today. Many people understand that God is at work in the death of Jesus. They understand that strange and mighty forces are being released in this remarkable event. They understand that he was more than a mere man, but it never gets further than that. They are impressed by the cross and impressed by the character of Jesus, but it never becomes personalized, and they never enter into the value of that death.

In verse 40, Mark describes a great crowd of women who were gathered about the cross.

> There were also women looking on from afar, among whom were Mary Magdalene, and Mary the mother of James the younger and of Joses, and Salome, who, when he was in Galilee, followed him, and ministered to him; and also many other women who came up with him to Jerusalem (Mk. 15:40–41).

Isn't it a strange thing that around the cross of Jesus gathered this crowd of women? Where were the men? Where were James and John—and Peter, with all his bluster—at this hour? John's Gospel tells us that John had been there; he had been there with Mary, the mother of Jesus, and they stood at the foot of the cross. In those first three hours Jesus had found time in the midst of his own suffering to commit his mother to the care of the disciple John. But evidently John was gone now. He had led Mary away, and only the women were left around the cross. Women—they were the first to love Jesus, and they were the last to stop loving him. That says something beautiful that I think is truly characteristic of women.

Are men and women simply human beings who are completely alike at the bottom, but simply come in two different models? That is a big question today, and I think this scene around the cross gives us a partial answer. Yes, there is a difference. The stark revelation of the clear light of the cross unveils exactly what is going on in human hearts. It reveals that women, who love first, who easily respond emotionally, are able also to maintain their love longer than men. This is a beautiful tribute to womanhood.

These women are not gathering around the cross in hope; they are gathering in hopelessness. This is a picture of hopeless commitment. It was the women who stayed with Jesus and tried to minister to his dead body, bringing spices to anoint him. The men were gone. There are many today who believe in God; they believe in the record of the Scripture. They believe that God is there and that he works—until it comes to the exact moment of a crisis in their own life. Then their hope is gone. They really have no hope that God actually will act in the hour of despair. While their love remains, their hope and faith are gone. Their faith is strong as long as everything goes well, but when the bottom drops out, they still love, but their faith is gone.

Mark relates one final scene:

> And when evening had come, since it was the day of Preparation, that is, the day before the sabbath, Joseph of Arimathea, a respected member of the council, who was also himself looking for the kingdom of God, took courage and went to Pilate, and asked for the body of Jesus. And Pilate wondered if he were already dead; and summoning the centurion, he asked him whether he was already dead. And when he learned from the centurion that he was dead, he granted the body to Joseph. And he bought a linen shroud, and taking him down, wrapped him in the linen shroud, and laid him in a tomb which had been hewn out of the rock; and he rolled a stone against the door of the tomb. Mary Magdalene and Mary the mother of Joses saw where he was laid (Mk. 15:42–47).

Here is Joseph of Arimathea, the secret disciple, a wealthy member of the Sanhedrin of Jerusalem, looking for the Kingdom of God. He was attracted toward Jesus, but he was afraid

to come out in the open. All through the record of the trial of
Jesus, there is never any sign of Joseph. He doesn't raise his
voice in the court where Jesus appeared before the Sanhedrin.
But after the death of the Lord, when the body was hanging
dead on the tree, Mark says Joseph took courage and finally
stood up to be counted.

A lot of us are like that. We are willing to go along with
our Christianity until it gets us into trouble or threatens us.
Then we resist and hide for a long time. But when the chips
are down, we stand up and say, "Yes, I'm with him too." Thank
God for Joseph who at last found the courage to stand up for
what he believed.

There are the hearts of the people around the cross, stripped
of all pretense and cover. The cross always removes all
hypocrisy and leaves us standing stark naked before God. In
the midst of this, Mark lists these three climactic events: First,
the cry from our Lord in the last three hours, when a mysterious,
strange darkness covered the face of the land. Emerging out
of that darkness came what has been called "Emanuel's or-
phaned cry": "Eloi, Eloi, lama sabach-thani, My God, my God,
why hast thou forsaken me?" Second, almost immediately after
the loud cry, Jesus dismissed his spirit—he didn't die, he dismissed his spirit. He wasn't put to death, he gave up his spirit;
he was obedient unto death. Finally, a half mile away in the
court of the temple, within the sacred enclosure of the holy
place, the huge veil that marked off the Holy of Holies where
only the high priest was permitted to enter once a year—that
great veil split from top to bottom. By an invisible hand it was
torn apart and split wide open until the Holy of Holies was
exposed to the gaze of the priests, one of whom perhaps told
Mark about it.

For sheer drama there is nothing like this in all of recorded
history. This cry in the darkness of the cross, the dismissing of
the spirit of Jesus, and the rending of the veil in the temple—
Mark brings them all together in order that we might under-

stand what these events mean. As Jesus' cry rang out, "My God, my God, why hast thou forsaken me?" there must have been many in the crowd who recognized that it was the opening words of the twenty-second Psalm. If you want to get the background and atmosphere of the cross, read that Psalm through. There is no adequate explanation for the question that Jesus asked except that which Scripture itself gives, notably in 2 Corinthians 5:21 where Paul says, "For our sake he made him to be sin who knew no sin, so that in him we might become the righteousness of God."

I don't think it is possible for any of us to even remotely understand the agony that wrung this tremendous cry from the lips of Jesus. If you can imagine a beautiful young girl, an innocent virgin, being raped by an ugly, foul, rapacious man, and the horror that she would feel in that moment, you aren't even in the range of what was going through the soul of Jesus when he was made sin for us. You say, "I don't understand it." Well, join the club—I am way beyond my depth in trying to explain anything about these events to you.

### No Revenge

Then there comes the loud cry of dismissal and the rending of the veil. Why did the veil split in two? It was God's dramatic way of saying for all time and for all people that the way into his heart is wide open. God is not planning revenge. All those who gathered around the cross in hatred and malice against Jesus—every one of them is welcome to come back. That is what the rent veil means. The penalty has been paid for the hateful, the cruel, the ignorant, the selfish, the empty-headed thrill seekers. The way is wide open and God is waiting to restore the hopeless, the helpless, the fearful.

When I was just a young Christian in my early twenties, I read a message by D. L. Moody that I have never forgotten. It was the great evangelist's imaginative description of what happened after Jesus rose from the dead. Moody says he gathered his disciples in Jerusalem and said to them, "Men, I want you to go and find the priests who mocked me, who hurled in my teeth the taunt, 'He saved others, himself he could not save.' Explain to them that if I had saved myself, they would have been doomed men. But tell them there is a way wide open." The book of Acts says that as Peter and the other disciples preached in Jerusalem, "a great company of priests were obedient unto the faith."

Moody said further that Jesus said to the disciples, "Go find the soldiers who cast lots for my garments, for my seamless robe, and tell them that there is a far greater treasure awaiting them if they will come to me. They shall have not a seamless robe, but a spotless heart. All their guilt can be washed away; all their callous cruelty can be forgiven if they come. Find the centurion who thrust his spear into my side and tell him there is a closer way to my heart if he will come, just as a sinner needing forgiveness."

In this beautiful scene of the rending of the veil at the moment of the death of Jesus, God is saying that the way to him is open to us, despite the attitudes we so frequently have had toward him. As Charles Wesley expressed it in his hymn:

'Tis mystery all! Th'Immortal dies!
Who can explore His strange design?
In vain the first-born seraph tries
To sound the depths of love Divine!
'Tis mercy all! let earth adore,
Let angel minds inquire no more.
Amazing love! How can it be
That Thou, my God, shouldst die for me!

# 16

# A Rumor of Hope

Dr. Carl F. Henry, one of America's leading contemporary theologians, said recently of Jesus, "He planted the only durable rumor of hope amid the widespread despair of a hopeless world." We come now to Mark's final, brief description of the events that have given rise to that "rumor."

And when the sabbath was past, Mary Magdalene, and Mary, the mother of James, and Salome, bought spices, so that they might go and anoint him. And very early on the first day of the week they went to the tomb when the sun had risen. And they were saying to one another, "Who will roll away the stone for us from the door of the tomb?" And looking up, they saw the stone was rolled back; for it was very large. And entering the tomb, they saw a young man sitting on the right side, dressed in a white robe; and they were amazed. And he said to them, "Do not be amazed; you seek Jesus of Nazareth, who was crucified. He has risen, he is not here; see the place where they laid him. But go, tell his disciples and Peter that he is going before you to Galilee; there you will see him, as he told you." And they went out and fled from the tomb, for trembling and astonishment had come upon them; and they said nothing to any one, for they were afraid (Mk. 16:1–8).

There Mark ends his story. The footnote in the Revised Standard Version gives another ending for this Gospel which we will look at in our final study. But there the best of the early manuscripts end Mark's account.

The chapter begins with the darkest day in human history— that black Saturday when Jesus lay in the grave. But it ends with the women who had come to the tomb leaving filled with such joy and awe and exploding hope that they dared not breathe a word of it to anyone. When the close of the passage says, "they were afraid," it would be a mistake to read it as though it means they were terrified or threatened, because they were not. The word for "astonishment" in the original Greek is literally "ecstasy." They were caught up in an ecstasy of excitement and trembling awe at what they heard from the angel in the tomb. It is this that sent them out to establish a rumor of hope in the midst of the hopelessness of mankind. Look with me to see what it was that made these women change so dramatically from despair to trembling joy.

The account opens with the words, "And when the sabbath was past . . ." The other Gospels do not mention the sabbath, but Mark gives us this brief account of it. That Saturday before the resurrection must have been the darkest day the disciples had ever experienced—a dreary, interminable day of shattered hopes, broken dreams, desolated spirits, and wounded, frightened hearts. This was a day in which the future was grim and foreboding. All their brightest hopes had collapsed around them; all their choicest dreams had perished with the death of Jesus. Every act on that day must have been torture for them, since they had no belief in the resurrection, with every fiber of their being crying out, "What's the use! Why go on?" It was a day they would never forget as long as they lived.

All of us have felt something of that at some time. And you

know, there are more human beings today who live constantly in the despair and hopelessness symbolized by that dark Saturday than have ever lived in the drama of Friday or the victory of Easter. Someone has called our present generation "Saturday's children," and it is an apt term. Our great American cities are, for the most part, teeming pools of human misery where people live out their days in a kind of ritual dance toward death without hope or illusion. In the midst of an increasingly godless world, despair grips people's hearts everywhere. Hopelessness and meaninglessness come crushing in on us from every side. Not even the most optimistic of the prophets and seers of today, either secular or sacred, in looking into the future see any hope in the affairs of men as they are. We are indeed Saturday's children.

And yet, the amazing thing about this account is that when the time came to record these events, when the proper hour arrived for these disciples to sit down and write their accounts, this dark day had so dropped into the background, was so lost in the joy of resurrection, that the most they felt it necessary to say was, "And when the sabbath was past . . ." Their joy had swallowed up their despair.

The first thing that gave these women hope was that the stone was rolled away from the tomb. They came concerned and worried about that stone. If you visit the Garden Tomb in Jerusalem where I think this event took place, you will see that the stone is no longer there, but you can see right in front of the tomb the narrow, grooved platform along which it was rolled. The entrance into the tomb itself is almost as tall as a man. The stone which covered the entrance to that tomb must have weighed at least a thousand pounds. It was indeed a very large stone, as the account tells us, and these women were naturally concerned about how to roll it away so that they might anoint the body of Jesus with the spices and ointments which they had brought. But when they arrived, the stone was already rolled back. Matthew tells us that very early, long before daybreak, an angel had come and rolled back the stone and sat upon it. His countenance was like lightening—bright and shining—so that he dazzled and dismayed the guards who had been detailed to watch over the tomb. They fell as dead men on the ground, and then, as they recovered their senses, they stumbled off into the darkness in fear. All of this had happened before the women arrived. When they came, there was no sign of anyone, and the door of the tomb was open, so they understood that something remarkable had occurred.

## No Explanations

Then, when they went into the tomb, the body of Jesus was gone. That which they had come to anoint was no longer there. This empty tomb has been the answer to all the arguments of skeptics for twenty centuries. No one has ever been able to explain it. Every generation has tried. In our own day we have Schonfield's *Passover Plot,* as one of the most recent attempts to explain away the events of the crucifixion and the resurrection. But it, like all the others, relies upon that ancient lie circulated in the very first century by the soldiers, who were paid to say that the friends of Jesus had come and stolen his body away. No one has ever been able to explain how that could happen. That his enemies would steal it is impossible to believe, because they would gladly have produced it. And that his friends could do it is impossible to conceive, for there were guards stationed at the tomb, and the stone was sealed with the Great Seal of Rome.

The most amazing thing of all, the thing that confronted these women as they went into the tomb, was the fact that though the body itself was gone, the grave clothes were still there, lying as though still wrapped around a body in the place where the body had been laid. The body seemingly had evaporated through the grave clothes; it was gone. It was evident that there was no body there, but the formation of the cloth was as though it were still wrapped around the body.

The other Gospels tell us that when these women left the tomb, they ran to the disciples and told them the news, and Peter and John came running to the tomb. When they went in and saw the grave clothes, they were convinced that Jesus indeed had risen. The fact of these grave clothes has never been explained. No one has ever satisfactorily explained the conundrums and puzzles which arise with regard to these empty grave clothes.

The words of the angel to these women contain the answer to all the skepticism of twenty centuries. For the angel said some things to them which answer most of the claims which have ever been raised in questioning the actuality of the resurrection. The first thing the angel said was, "This Jesus of Nazareth, this One who was crucified, this same one whom you seek, has indeed risen from the dead." Many of the attempts to explain this away say that the women went to the wrong tomb, or that they found the wrong person, or that the disciples invented another person—not the same Jesus. They say that the Jesus who lived and walked through the pages of the Gospels was crucified and lies yet in some unknown Syrian grave—as Matthew Arnold put it, "Upon his grave, with shining eyes, the Syrian stars look down. . . ." That whole question is answered here by the angel. He says to the women, "This very same Jesus, the One you knew from Nazareth, whom you accompanied about the hills of Galilee and Judea, the Jesus who was crucified, whom you saw on the cross with the nails in his hands and the blood running down his side, that same One whom you are seeking, is risen from the dead." That establishes the identity of Jesus.

Then he said to them, "He is not here." That is, "He is not only risen; he is not here." And in those words he makes very clear that though Jesus is risen, there is, nevertheless, a very real tie with our humanity. He is not just a spirit. This is not a spiritual but a bodily resurrection. It was the body of Jesus that rose from the dead. There are cults and groups today that try to argue against that, who claim that what happened was that the spirit of Jesus rose, and he now lives spiritually only. But the Bible consistently defends the proposition that it was the very body which was put into the grave, dead, which also rose from the dead. "He is not here." He is a person yet, a human person with a human body—changed, yes—but still human. And in that human body he rose from the dead. That is the claim of Scripture. "Furthermore," the angel said, "he goes before you to Galilee." In other words, there is a specific geographical spot on the face of the earth, that you well know, where you will see him. He will be there when you get there. "Go and tell his disciples that he goes before you to Galilee." So the angel underscores the claims of Scripture that Jesus is alive, that he rose bodily, and that he is available in specific places.

The third thing the angel says is put in these extraordinary words that only Mark records: "But go, tell his disciples and *Peter* that he is going before you to Galilee." That is a wonderful touch. What a gentle, tender word that is! The last time we saw Peter in this Gospel account, he was weeping bitterly in the darkness of the night after denying his Lord three times. What a tender thing it is for the angel to say to these women, "Go and tell the disciples *and Peter* that he goes before you to Galilee." This puts him right back into the apostolic band.

## The Most Intimate Communion

What this says to us is that Jesus is available to individuals —not just to the crowd at large, not just to the world in general, or the church, but to you and me. Put your own name in there if you like. This accessibility to individuals has been the hallmark of Christianity ever since. Each one of us can know him personally, intimately—not just as a figure of history, nor as a coming King, nor in a general sense, as we know about the President of the United States, but in that intimate, personal, real, conscious sense of knowing, which we share in the most intimate communion of men.

The last thing the angel said was, "He is going before you to Galilee; there you will see him, *as he told you.*" That is, these are faithful words. Jesus had already promised that he would do this. This ought not to have taken them by surprise because he had said that he would go before them to Galilee when he rose from the dead—there he would meet them. The angel is underscoring the reliability of the words of Jesus. He is absolutely trustworthy; he does what he says he will do. His promises can be believed. Whatever he said, he also fulfilled, and you can rely upon it to the very last letter.

This is what changed these women. This is what filled them with hope, brought them from the very depths of dark despair to trembling ecstasy, so that they went out with gladness to spread this rumor of hope throughout the world—the only durable rumor of hope that the world has ever known.

You are familiar with the story—how the Gospel accounts tell us that just a few moments later, as Mary Magdalene lingered behind there in the early morning light, Jesus appeared to her. At first she thought he was the gardener, but when he spoke her name, she knew who he was. He showed himself alive first of all to Mary. She went running with the news, and Peter and John came to the tomb and saw the grave clothes and were convinced. Then in the afternoon he appeared on the road to Emmaus to two disciples, and that strange encounter took place where he walked with them and opened the Scriptures to them and taught them from the Scriptures about himself. And then that evening in the upper room, where ten of the disciples were gathered together, Jesus suddenly stood in their midst and showed himself alive to them.

Jesus had said to go to Galilee, and there they would see him. I think that is referring to the intimate account which John gives us, where on the beach of the Sea of Galilee, Jesus says to Peter, "Peter, do you love me?" Peter answers, "You know I do, Lord." Again, "Peter, do you love me?" "Yes, Lord; you know that I love you." And yet a third time, "Peter, do you love me?" And Peter cried, "Lord, you know everything; you know that I love you." Then Jesus gave him his commission: "Feed my sheep." He was to be a pastor, a shepherd to the flock of God, which Peter took as his lifelong work from that time on. This was why the angel sent that personal word to Peter when he spoke to the women at the tomb.

Then we are told that one week later, still in Jerusalem, Jesus appeared to the eleven disciples when Thomas the doubter was invited to touch him, feel the scars, and was convinced by that. Paul tells us further that he appeared to more than five hundred people at one time on a mountain in Galilee. Then, back in Bethany, Jesus appeared for the last time and led his disciples from Bethany to the Mount of Olives. And from the top of that mountain, as they were talking together, they watched him ascend into the heavens and disappear behind a cloud; they saw him no longer.

## Not Having Seen

The point that Mark makes here is that these women believed, even though they did not see. How wonderful to have been able to see the risen Lord! All those who did so were regarded after that with unusual respect and awe in the Christian community. But not all were privileged to do that. When Jesus appeared to Thomas the doubter and invited him to feel the wounds in his hands and side, he said to him, "Thomas, because you have seen, you believe; but blessed are those who have not seen, and yet believe." In these words he was looking down through the course of the ages since and including us all when he said, "Blessed are those who, having not seen, yet believe." Peter writes something similar: "Without having seen him you love him; though you do not now see him you believe in him and rejoice with unutterable and exalted joy" (1 Pet. 1:8).

That has been the experience of thousands, even millions, from that day on. That is where we are today. We have not seen the risen Lord. He left the realm of the visibilities of earth many centuries ago. But we have the testimony. We have this evidence—these many infallible proofs of which Luke speaks, which are convincing to the intellect and encouraging to the emotions to awaken hope within us, as these women found their hope awakened by the word of the angel.

This brings us to the final point: if there is an invitation to this risen Lord to enter into your life and heart, you too will know him, feel him, have him present in your life. Have you learned to worship the risen Lord? Have you found him to come into your heart and life and change you? That is what makes life different. That is what puts joy in a heart and a smile on a face. That is what makes Christianity really Christianity. It is but an empty ritual, mere religious dogma, without the experience of a living, risen Lord.

I want to share with you an account sent to me by Jay Kessler, president of Youth for Christ, International. He said,

> I've never seen a clearer example of the miracle of God's resurrection power than in the life of Lonnie Chapman. When Lonnie was a child, he stole from the grocery store because his parents refused to give him food. He was beaten, locked up, and cursed by his alcoholic father. When he was twelve, he watched his father rape his ten-year-old sister. Once his father tried to kill him with a piece of timber. Once his father punished him by breaking his fingers with a brick.
>
> Lonnie survived. He dropped out of school, traveled around, and ended up in California, where he teamed up with a friend whose name was Galen. Galen helped him become a thief and a murderer. After nearly half a dozen filling station stick-ups, Galen, Lonnie, and another teen robbed a California filling station. They kidnapped the attendant to keep him from calling the police. They drove him out into the country and tied him up with electrical cord. At that moment, Lonnie relates, Galen

went into an insane rage and yelled, "Kill him Lonnie, kill him!" According to Lonnie, he didn't want to do it. He fired the rifle at the ground below the victim's feet. Galen screamed, "You didn't kill him, you didn't kill him!" Trembling, afraid for his own life, Lonnie walked up to the helpless victim and shot him. A rifle blast in the face and another in the lower back ended his life.

Lonnie is in prison now, sentenced to a life term for first degree murder. I don't want to say Lonnie's tragedy happened only because Galen influenced him, but the influence was there.

Later, sitting in prison, Lonnie met a different kind of friend —Rod Burke, one of the Youth for Christ staff who spoke to him through a radio broadcast. Lonnie wrote to Rod, and Rod quickly drove over to see him with a gift copy of the New Testament under his arm. Young teens, Christians, began to back up Rod's prison visits with fervent prayer. Lonnie read that New Testament from cover to cover. Today, in Lonnie's probation report, you'll find this curious and cautiously worded sentence: "From conversations with the defendant, and letters from several other sources, it appears that the defendant has, in fact, undergone the Christian conversion experience." What an enormous understatement! Even in his prison cell you can see that Lonnie is an utterly transformed young man. He has inner peace. He is forgiven. He is without bitterness. He knows that he may spend the rest of his days in prison, and yet he has found meaning and purpose in his life. He witnesses before his fellow prisoners. He has given New Testaments to all his cellmates. He writes letters to people he believes he can help. Ask him, and he'll tell you that he has been born anew to a living hope, through the resurrection of Jesus Christ. And it's enough. It's all he needs, even in a prison cell.

Jesus is alive. Jesus is available. Jesus will do what he says. He will fulfill his promise. And this is his promise: "If anyone hears my voice, and opens the door [the door of your heart], I will enter into him and live with him, and he with me." That is his promise, and he does what he says he will do. Millions today are finding out this great fact—that he can change a life and, despite the circumstances, even if they are bleak and despairing, he can fill the heart with joy and peace and glory and make you over again.

If you have not yet found the peace and joy and forgiveness and hope that a living Lord Jesus, living with you in your life and heart, can bring to your life, just ask, "Lord Jesus, come into my life." Open the door to him, say, "Come in, fill me, take me." You may have been religious, you may have been raised in a Christian home, and still have not found the living Lord. His presence is what makes the difference between death and life, darkness and light.

# 17

# Those Signs Following

I suppose one of the most controversial movements in the church today is the one called the charismatic movement. I do not like to use the word "charismatic" for a movement that stresses just one or two gifts of the Spirit, for all the gifts of the Spirit are charismatic. In 1 Corinthians 12 the apostle Paul clearly says that every Christian has one or more charis matic gifts. I would prefer to call this group we are observing in the church now the Pentecostal movement, or, perhaps even more accurately, the glossolalia movement. The term "glossolalia" comes from the Greek (*glossa*, the tongue, and *lalia*, to speak), and it is the more accurate term for this group because it stresses speaking in tongues. This movement relies heavily upon the closing verses of Mark's Gospel for biblical support of its views. These verses refer to the signs that accompany those who believe: casting out demons, speaking in new tongues, healing the sick, picking up serpents, drinking poison, etc. We want to examine this passage very carefully now.

In some versions, particularly the Revised Standard Version, you find these verses in a footnote at the bottom of the page. That is because many scholars are in doubt as to whether these

verses actually belong to the Gospel of Mark. It is true that
the best of the Greek manuscripts do not contain these twelve
verses, but it is also true that the overwhelming majority of
the Greek manuscripts that we have today do contain these
verses. And it is also true that two of the earliest church fathers,
writing from the beginning of the second century, quote from
this passage. So it is clear that from the very beginning the
church has accepted these twelve verses as accurate, even
though they may not have come from the hand of Mark.

In this passage you will note one immediate change from
the rest of the Gospel: it is not in narrative form. Up to this
point, Mark has been narrating in sequence the events as they
happened to Jesus, bringing us right up to the stirring events
of the crucifixion and resurrection. This last section, however,
does not narrate events. It summarizes in brief order the events
that occurred over a period of about forty days, and that change
to summary form does indicate that perhaps it was written by
a person other than Mark.

The key to this passage is the word "believe," which is in
line with the thrust of Mark's Gospel. Mark does not present
Christianity as just a nice story, a fascinating account of events
that took place in the first century. He stresses the fact that
the death and resurrection of Christ is something to be believed, and it is intended to change lives. As we act on our belief, it changes us. The emphasis here is on the belief of these
apostles whom Jesus was to send out into all the world with
this great story.

If you want a simple division of the passage, the first verses,
9–14, deal with the basis of apostolic belief; verses 15 and 16
deal with the apostolic preaching; and the rest of the passage,
verses 16–20, deals with the confirmation of the apostolic
witness.

Let's examine first the basis of apostolic belief:

Now when he rose early on the first day of the week, he appeared first to Mary Magdalene, from whom he had cast out

seven demons. She went and told those who had been with him, as they mourned and wept. But when they heard that he was alive and had been seen by her, they would not believe it (Mk. 16:9–11).

Immediately, the writer underscores the fact that these disciples, when they heard of Mary's experience with Jesus, did not believe it. You remember how the women had come to the tomb early in the morning, at the first light of dawn, and found the stone rolled away and saw the angel. The angel told them what had happened. "He is risen, as he said," But they did not see Jesus then. Mary Magdalene, according to John's account, was ahead of the others and, seeing the empty tomb, she ran to tell Peter and John immediately. Evidently, she did not hear the angel's explanation. Peter and John both ran to the tomb. Peter went inside and saw the graveclothes lying there still wrapped as though they were around a body, and the cloth that had been on Jesus' head was folded and placed aside. This convinced Peter and John that indeed Jesus was risen, but they still had not seen him. Mary Magdalene returned more slowly to the tomb and, John tells us, as she stood weeping in the garden and saw what she thought was the gardener, she asked him where they had laid the body of Jesus. He spoke her name, and she knew it was Jesus; holding him by the feet, she worshiped him. This was the first appearance of the risen Lord to a disciple. He came first, as we read here, to Mary Magdalene. But when she told the other disciples that Jesus was alive and that she had actually seen him, they would not believe it.

## More Unbelief

In verse 13, Jesus appears to two disciples: "After this he appeared in another form to two of them, as they were walking into the country. And they went back and told the rest, but they did not believe them."

Here we have a reference to the account Luke gives of the two disciples who were walking some eleven miles to the little

village of Emmaus. Jesus appeared in "another form," Mark
explains, and they did not know him. This was an extended
conversation; as they walked along, he began with Moses and
the prophets and showed them all the things that referred to
Messiah. But it was not until they sat at table with him and saw
his hands as he broke bread that they recognized their crucified
Lord. Then he disappeared.

These two disciples came back to Jerusalem immediately and
told the eleven what they had seen, but even the eleven did
not believe them.

> Afterward he appeared to the eleven themselves as they sat at
> table; and he upbraided them for their unbelief and hardness of
> heart, because they had not believed those who saw him after
> he had risen (Mk. 16:14).

Mark wants us to understand what a climate of persistent
and stubborn unbelief prevailed among these disciples after
the resurrection. They found it difficult to accept the amazing
fact that the one they had seen crucified was now risen and was
living among them again. The significant thing here is that
Jesus himself expected the eleven to believe before they saw
him. He wanted and expected them to believe the reports of
the eyewitnesses who had seen him. They were trustworthy
persons and were reporting what they themselves had actually
experienced, and that should have been enough to convince
these disciples that Jesus was risen from the dead. So concerned
is he about this that he rebukes them. Even as he did in the
days of his flesh, so now he, as their living, risen Lord, rebukes
them for their unbelief. He takes them to task because they refused to believe those who had seen him.

You can see the importance he attributes to this matter of
believing eyewitnesses. John's Gospel tells us that a week later
Jesus appeared to them when Thomas, who had not been with
them when he appeared the first time, was present. Jesus in-

vited Thomas to examine him, to put his hand on his side and touch the nail-prints in his hands and feet. Thomas did so and fell down at his feet, crying, "My Lord and my God!" Jesus said, "Have you believed because you have seen me? Blessed are those who have not seen and yet believe." Years later, when Peter is writing his letters to the Christians, he says to them, "Without having seen him you love him; though you do not now see him you believe in him and rejoice with unutterable and exalted joy" (1 Pet. 1:8). When we have adequate, trustworthy witnesses who report to us what they have seen, we are expected to respond with belief. These men saw the risen Lord. They were granted a privilege that we are not granted; but, nevertheless, our faith can rest upon solid foundation. We believe even though we've not seen him because of the eyewitness accounts here. Now, remember the disciples' struggle to believe in the resurrection because that is the climate in which the rest of this passage dealing with the "signs following" is given.

After rebuking the disciples for their unbelief, Jesus gives them a command:

> And he said to them, "Go into all the world and preach the gospel to the whole creation. He who believes and is baptized will be saved; but he who does not believe will be condemned" (Mk. 16:15–16).

Amazingly, the translators of this passage have always handled it as though Jesus was emphasizing the word "go." That is not the central command he gave to these disciples. In both Matthew and Mark, where we have the great commission, what we should emphasize is "preach," for this is the command. It should read like this: "As you go into all the world (that is taken for granted), preach the good news to the whole creation." Our Lord takes it for granted that the church will grow and develop throughout all the world, and it is right that we should think about how to reach out to the world. I am not diminishing the emphasis on missions at all. But I want to point out that the instruction our Lord gives is that while we are going, we are to preach, to tell the good news.

## No Mention of Heaven

Now the good news, clearly, is the death and resurrection of Jesus himself. Nothing can be clearer than that. The good news is not that Jesus came to earth; the good news is that he died and rose again. The implications of those events and what they mean to us—that is the good news! For in the death of Jesus you have the solution of the terrible problem of human evil—the force that grips us and destroys all our good intentions. That force is finally destroyed, vitiated, by the death of Jesus. The implication of the resurrection is that Jesus himself, the same Jesus that lived and talked and manifested his life and power on the hills of Judea and Galilee, that same Jesus can now live within us and is available to us. He will live again that same life, in terms of our circumstances, right where we are. That is the incredible good news of the gospel. There is no mention of the fact that when you die you will go to heaven. That is certainly part of the good news. But, almost invariably, heaven is what people think you are talking about when you mention the good news. They think it is some way to get past death. Heaven is not the good news; it is but a result of the good news. The good news is that the power of evil in your life and mine can be broken! It no longer grips us and ruins everything we try to do. It is broken by the power of the resurrection of Jesus. The living Lord himself lives within us and imparts to us power to act. This is the good news, and this is what we ought to be telling abroad.

Christianity without the death and resurrection of Jesus is pablum that is handed out to people as a kind of moral teaching—which, since it is impossible for them to follow, is therefore useless. Mark Twain used to say, "It isn't the parts of the

Bible I can't understand that bother me; it's the parts I do understand." Men do not need to be told what to do. What they need is to be changed, to be altered at the very depths of their being so they can do what they already know is right. That is what Scripture calls salvation. That is why Jesus said, "He who believes (this good news) and is baptized will be saved; but he who does not believe will be condemned."

There are some who quibble over the word "baptism." Certain groups today take this word, press it to an unwarranted extreme, and say it is necessary not only to believe but also to be baptized in order to be saved. Such an extreme is totally unsupported by the rest of Scripture, however. What Jesus means is that belief ought to be real, and the reality of that inward belief is demonstrated by the outward action of baptism. Only that belief which changes us and makes us act is real belief, and the way we can demonstrate it is by being baptized. But that does not add to what the belief itself has already accomplished; it only demonstrates it. If you cannot be baptized, that does not affect your salvation at all. God knows and reads the heart. But ordinarily, belief is to be translated into action by this ritual which is designed to express faith in Jesus Christ and says in very eloquent terms that you have been put down into death and risen again to walk with him in newness of life.

I have found people who dislike this word "saved" because it makes them feel uncomfortable. Well, I understand that. There have been times when I have felt uncomfortable when people used this term. For somebody to rush up to me, grab me by the lapels, and say, "Brother, are you saved?" always turns me off. It is not so much the term as the way it is used that turns people off. But I think it is clear that those who struggle with this word have never really understood the hopelessness of humanity. Once you begin to see how absolutely helpless you are to change your pattern of life, to be acceptable to God apart from the work of Jesus Christ, you will understand what "saved" means. Then you will know that this is the only

possible word that could have been used—that mankind indeed
is like a drowning man, hopeless and helpless, unless somebody
rescues him. As someone has well put it,

> Your best resolutions must wholly be waived,
> Your highest ambitions be crossed;
> You need never think that you'll ever be saved,
> Until you have learned that you're lost.

When you come to the place of learning how helpless you are,
then this word of release comes in with mighty, thrilling, hope-
giving power: "Believe and be saved."

Now, just because salvation reduces man to having nothing
to offer God, we struggle with it. We do not like that, therefore, it is frequently resisted and attacked and ridiculed. This
is especially true of the resurrection of Jesus, upon which our
faith rests. No part of Christianity has ever been subjected to
more severe ridicule, more clever attack, than the resurrection.
In every generation it is under attack because, as Paul put it,
"If Jesus Christ be not risen from the dead, then our faith is
in vain."

Knowing the pressure that would be brought against these
apostles to get them to deny this supernatural event, our Lord
now goes on to give them certain signs which will accompany
and encourage them in preaching the gospel. This climate of
unbelief is the setting:

> "And these signs will accompany those who believe: In my
> name they will cast out demons; they will speak in new tongues;
> they will pick up serpents, and if they drink any deadly thing, it
> will not hurt them; they will lay their hands on the sick, and
> they will recover" (Mk. 16:17–18).

It is easy to read this as though Jesus means these signs will
accompany everyone who believes and preaches the gospel.
Unfortunately, the text makes it appear this way, and this is

how this passage has been understood by many. As you go about preaching the gospel, these signs will immediately confirm that the faith of those who believe is genuine. But the amazing fact is that for twenty centuries millions of people have been converted and have believed the gospel and none of these signs have appeared. There have been claims that these signs have been manifested in certain instances, but if this is what these words meant, then these signs would be everywhere. Some of these signs would be manifested every time a person became a Christian. Therefore, they ought to be the most frequent occurrence in all Christendom. But the truth is: they are very rarely, if ever, seen. Now what does this mean? Well, it means of course that we have misunderstood this passage if we read it that way. It does not square with what God actually does.

## In the Face of Hostility

I think there is a rather simple solution to the problem. If we put the passage back in its context, in terms of the climate of unbelief which prevailed among these disciples as the word about the resurrection was brought to them, then we see that Jesus is addressing these words not to those who believe the gospel but to these disciples who believed or disbelieved in his resurrection. When he says to them, "These signs will accompany those who believe," he is speaking about the disciples. I think we can even insert these words, "those [among you] who believe," without doing violence to the text. Jesus is saying to these disciples, "Now go and preach in all creation. And to encourage you, in the face of the hostility you will encounter, certain signs that only God could do will accompany you." They would be given power to deliver from demons, power to set free from demonic influence. They would be given power to praise God in a new language.

The term "new tongues" means speaking in a language that hasn't been learned. The disciples would be given this ability as a means of praising God. Paul himself tells us in 1 Corinthians 12 that he who speaks in a tongue does not speak to man. I do not know why it is so hard for us to accept that fact. Everywhere people consider tongues as a means of speaking to men—of preaching the gospel or of conveying messages or prophesying events. And yet Paul says he who speaks in a tongue does not speak to men but to God. He goes on to make clear that speaking in tongues is an act of praise and thanksgiving to God for his magnificent works among men and as a sign to unbelievers. You remember these two things are underscored very strongly in Paul's great treatment of this in 1 Corinthians 14. "New tongues" are not spoken to men, but to God. And they are not for believers; they are a sign for unbelievers. Thus these disciples were sent out with this sign. I do not think this sign was limited to the apostles; others received the gift as well.

Further, the disciples would have power to survive physical attacks upon their lives. If bitten by a poisonous serpent, they would not die. If they accidentally drank poison, they would not die. They would have power to survive in order for the gospel to go out. This would be one of the authenticating signs given to them. This has nothing to do with the practices of certain Kentucky mountain people who handle rattlesnakes and drink strychnine as evidence of their faith. Actually, if you investigate those practices, you will find that they really affirm a lack of faith on their part, for periodically, one or more of them die as a result of having been bitten by a rattlesnake or by drinking poison. This is not what the gospel is talking about.

The fourth sign is power to heal—to lay hands upon the sick and they will recover. This was to be the invariable rule; the disciples would lay hands on the sick and 100 percent of them would recover. Again, you can see what a far cry this is from what we are seeing today in "healing services" that claim to fulfill this.

## Authenticating Signs

The apostle Paul did all these things. He cast out demons in the name of the Lord Jesus. He spoke in new tongues more than them all, he said, as praise and thanksgiving to God. I think he did it in the synagogue; it was not a private practice of his at home. When he was accidentally bitten by a poisonous snake, as recorded in the last chapter of Acts, he shook it off into the fire, unharmed, to the amazement of those who watched. He had power to lay hands on the sick, and they were healed; and he did it again and again. This is what he means when he writes, "the signs of a true apostle were performed among you in all patience, with signs and wonders and mighty works" (2 Cor. 12:12). These, then, are the signs of an apostle. They were authenticating signs to accompany those who first went out with the gospel into an unbelieving and hostile world. We have this confirmed, I think, by the final paragraph:

So then the Lord Jesus, after he had spoken to them, was taken up into heaven, and sat down at the right hand of God. And they went forth and preached everywhere, while the Lord worked with them [the disciples] and confirmed the message by the signs that attended it (Mk. 16:19-20).

Thus, the authentication was given to their ministry, and encouragement was given to their faith. We have another reference to this in the letter to the Hebrews where, in chapter 2, the writer reminds us,

. . . how shall we escape if we neglect such a great salvation? It was declared at first by the Lord, and it was attested to us by those who heard him, while God also bore witness by signs and wonders and various miracles and by gifts of the Holy Spirit distributed according to his own will (Heb. 2:3-4).

So Mark closes this gospel of his with the Lord in heaven—
not far off in space somewhere but in the invisible dimensions
of life right here among us, living as Lord in the midst of his
church, directing its events, planning its strategy, carrying it
unto the farthest reaches of the world. And the apostles, scattered throughout the known world of that day, preached this
good news, and their witness was confirmed by these great signs.
They, thus, laid the foundation of the great building that Paul
calls the church, the body of Christ, that has grown through all
the centuries since. Remember how in Ephesians 2 Paul says
that the foundation was laid by the apostles and the prophets,
Christ Jesus himself being the chief cornerstone upon which
the whole building grows (and has grown now for these twenty
centuries) into a habitation of God through the Spirit. That
foundation was laid by these apostles who speak to us the
truth about Jesus.

When you hear all these claims about Jesus today, are you
ever tempted to say, as I am, "Will the real Jesus please stand
up?" He does in these Scriptures. The real Jesus is the apostolic
Jesus, the one the apostles witnessed. And that witness is
underscored and confirmed by these signs which accompanied
them in their ministry so we would know that what they say
is the truth. May God grant that our work will rest upon this
great foundation that has already been laid and which no man
can re-lay. May we proclaim the good news of Jesus Christ,
alive, vital, ready to live within men and women to change our
lives, and to lead us into liberty, for that is what the gospel is
all about.

Thank you, our heavenly Father, for the good, good news that
Jesus Christ is not dead but alive, and that he lives within our
hearts and has the power to break the chains of sin, the bondage
of evil, in our lives. Thank you, Father, for the changes that
come as a result, the differences that he makes as he comes into
human hearts. And thank you for these apostles, these mighty

men who faithfully preached this great truth against much persecution and ridicule, and who clearly and accurately conveyed to us the facts upon which our faith rests. We pray that we may be faithful like them, and rest our faith upon this unchanging witness. We ask in Jesus' name, Amen.